PRESENTS

46th Edition

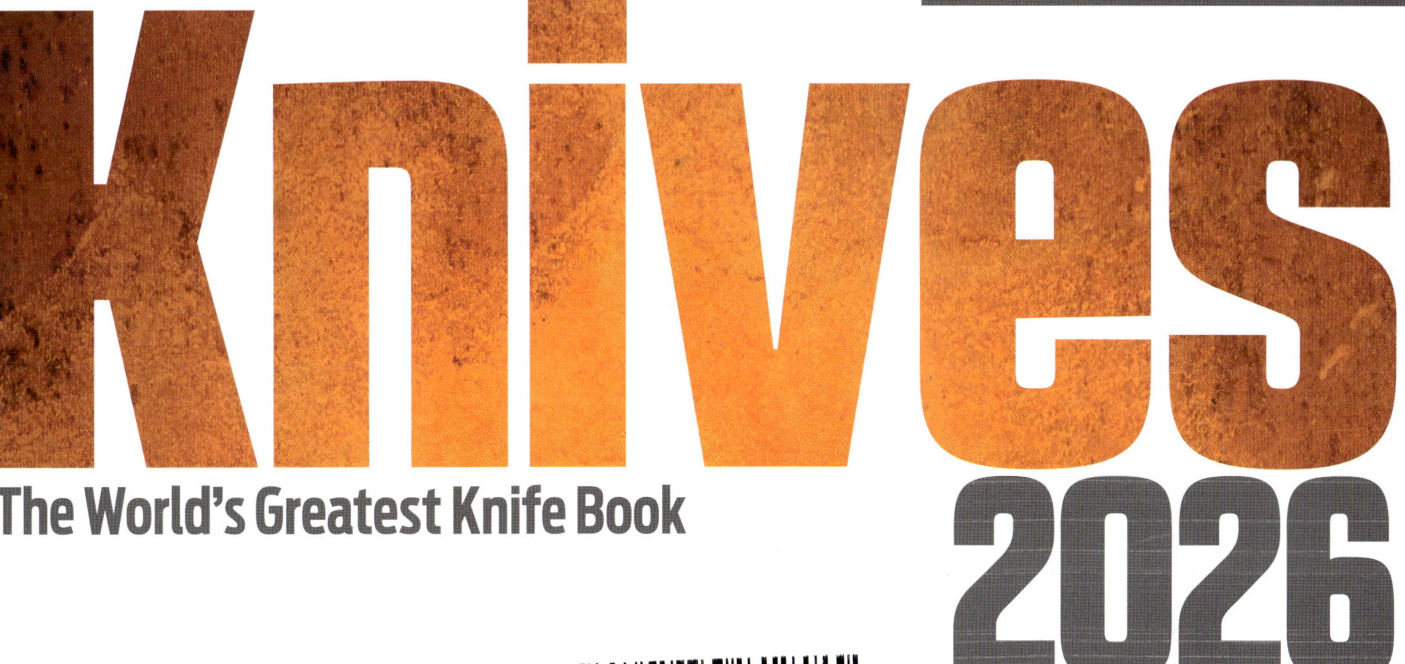

The World's Greatest Knife Book

2026

EDITED BY
JOE KERTZMAN

Published by

Gun Digest® Books, an imprint of Caribou Media Group, LLC
Gun Digest Media
5583 W. Waterford Ln., Suite D
Appleton WI 54913
gundigest.com

To order books or other products call 920.471.4522 ext. 104
or visit us online at gundigeststore.com

CAUTION: Technical data presented here, particularly technical data on handloading and on firearms adjustment and alteration, inevitably reflects individual experience with particular equipment and components under specific circumstances the reader cannot duplicate exactly. Such data presentations therefore should be used for guidance only and with caution. Caribou Media accepts no responsibility for results obtained using these data.

ISBN: 978-1-959265-49-8

Edited by Joe Kertzman and Corey Graff
Designed by Jong Cadelina
Cover design by Gene Coo

Printed in the United States of America

10 9 8 7 6 5 4 3 2 1

Dedication and Acknowledgments

Inevitably, at banquets across the world, when the recipient of a particular award, trophy or recognition steps up to the podium to accept the honor, they start thanking people who've helped them get to where they are, tutored them, and made their jobs easier. They recognize those who were sources of inspiration, provided financial backing or valuable information, researched and gathered data in the background, swept floors, did the heavy lifting, or sealed the final deals. In the end, there seems to be a common thread—they thank their spouses, significant others and family members. "Without them," they say, "I wouldn't be where I am today. I couldn't have done it without them."

Even actors and actresses who have landed Academy Awards and professional athletes who have just won the championship game start listing those they'd like to recognize. "I want to thank the Academy, my agent, fellow actors, and my mom. Without my mother's constant encouragement and all the sacrifices she made, I wouldn't be accepting this award tonight," is a typical acceptance speech. "I would first like to thank my Lord, Jesus Christ, who is all-powerful and giving. I want to thank my wife who raised the kids while I was flying across the country in pursuit of a career," is another paraphrased podium delivery.

When Steve Shackleford asked me if I'd do the honors of introducing A.G. Russell as the winner of a *BLADE Magazine* Knife of the Year® award that A.G. Russell Knives took home one year, I recalled a conversation I had with A.G. a few months earlier. A.G. confided in me that he regretted all the time he spent away from his wife, Goldie, and kids when he was on the road buying and selling knives and building a successful business. At first, I ribbed A.G. a little, telling the awards banquet audience I didn't have the heart to tell him I'd heard that same regret from many old drunken men sitting at bars. Then I gave him the credit he deserved, reminding him that he had a beautiful, smart, nice and successful family, and that one of his grandkids had even attended the BLADE Show with him that year and was in the audience. Of course, A.G. thanked his family when he got to the stage.

There's so much truth in the notion of spouses and children providing the motivation for one to do well in their chosen career. When I compare my bachelor days to the 30 years I've been married, the single guy was far less responsible than the husband and father. It's much different caring for oneself than having others in your care. When a child you've helped bring into the world suddenly needs new shoes, lunch money, funds for a field trip, braces for their teeth or a coat for the winter, there's no hitting the town and spending every cent you have on booze, cigars and T-bone steaks, not if you want to stay married and set a good example.

I always figured that all the hijinks I participated in when I was young would somehow be forgiven if I raised good kids. While my wife, Tricia, and I were raising our son and daughter, Danny and Cora, we decided that all we wanted was for them to be nice, successful and happy. But as they got older, I realized there was one other thing I wanted for them. It's something they taught me, or reminded me of, and that's to be excited about life. I never wanted them to lose the enthusiasm or wonder at the world around them.

I decided right there and then, after observing their youthful exuberance, that I'd never become a crabby old man complaining about gas prices, how the music I listened to as a teenager was better than anything made today, how young people couldn't have survived in my day, or how the whole world was falling apart. I'd never obsess over the television news, focus on politics, bemoan the fact that technology was ruining the planet or complain about the price of a gallon of milk, carton of eggs, or ohm of electricity.

I promised myself I'd never lose my own wonder and awe, that I'd choose to be happy, remain enthusiastic about the world around me and look forward to all the fun plans I had for that day and far into the future. I have my wife and kids to thank for that, so I acknowledge them and dedicate the *KNIVES 2026* book to Tricia, Danny and Cora. You are such nice, successful, happy and enthusiastic human beings, and I'm so proud of you.

Contents

On The Cover

What a lineup of knives! From left to right on the front cover are a **Carlos Queiros** "Thorn-TRS" model featuring a flat-ground "Odin's Eye" Damasteel blade, titanium hardware, and vintage canvas Micarta handle scales; a **Gavin Hawk** out-the-front auto with beautiful color engraving by **Wilfred Valtakis II**; **Peter Johnsson's** "Phosphoros Sword" in an organic chatoyance-pattern damascus blade, sterling silver guard, and a reindeer leather-wrapped wood hilt; a sleek **Gabe Fletcher** and **Don Nguyen** tuna sword-inspired slicer parading a long double-beveled damascus blade, an ivory G10 handle and carbon-fiber frame; **Javier Vogt's** "DRACO" guard-release auto in **Bertie Rietveld** fracture-pattern damascus, a hot-blued guard, blackened zirconium bolsters, and mammoth bark handle scales; and a **CobraTec** "Molon Labe" out-the-frontpartially serrated auto showcasing an aluminum alloy handle. At top-right is a folder resulting from a collaboration between **Jared Oeser** and **Michael Quesenberry** with gorgeous damascus blades and bolsters and pristine pearl handle scales, the latter including black-lip inserts. *(SharpByCoop and Jocelyn Frasier photos of the handmade knives)*

Introduction

Quality craftsmanship. Think about that term for a minute by closing your eyes and picturing everything that surrounds you—cars, furniture, kitchen appliances, clothing, stereophonics, campers, gear of any kind, equipment, desks, cabinets, wall hangings and even modern tools—how much of it can be defined as quality craftsmanship? Can your computer or iPhone be considered built to last, or how about the lighting fixtures and even the bulbs in your home, kids' toys, couches, flooring, curtains, shirts and shoes? If you're lucky, perhaps you've spent the money, researched, and purchased a few quality items here or there that will last a lifetime with little wear and tear.

If you've ever read the autobiographical book *Zen and the Art of Motorcycle Maintenance* by Robert M. Pirsig, you're aware that the author nearly drove himself to the brink of insanity trying to define the word "quality" and obsessing over the fact that there are so few things, especially motorcycles, in the modern world built from quality materials and workmanship. The bestselling novel was released in 2005, written over 20 years ago. Has quality craftsmanship improved since then?

Fortunately, as a reader of the *KNIVES 2026* book, you don't need to drive yourself to the brink of insanity, obsessing over the lack of quality craftsmanship in the world. More than a thousand examples are pictured herein, fashioned by some of the world's most talented knifemakers. Somewhere along the line, a group of skilled craftsmen and women toiling in the knife arena made the conscious decision to fashion quality cutting tools, from the blades, bolsters and guards to handles, pommels and sheaths. Whether driven by creative urges, pride or responsibility, bladesmiths and makers of everything sharp took it upon themselves to improve quality craftsmanship in the modern world.

Many began by pounding out rough blades from old rasps and files, leaf springs, and billets or bars of steel. They taught themselves or were mentored in heat treating, forging, quenching, shaping steel, grinding, honing and finishing. Some were born with the skills, and others developed the skillset. After years of practice perfecting the art of knifemaking, many turned their attention toward artistic embellishments, damascus pattern making, forging mosaic damascus, materials sourcing, leatherwork, purpose-driven holster manufacture and even parts making. Yes, some create their own pins, turn screws, and fashion springs, locks and liners.

Not just anyone can learn the arts of engraving, scrimshaw, steel sculpting, jewel inlaying, or carving, and pull it off. Most human beings in the world who'd attempt to scrimshaw lifelike figures in ancient or faux ivory would end up with stick figures and distorted forms that look amateurish at best. Few would succeed in catching the eyes of collectors of quality craftsmanship who have discerning tastes and the means to purchase works of functional art. That's another layer—the art in this case, a knife, must function, cut, pierce, slash, remain sharp and wear well. Military, police or fire and rescue knives can't fail, and few construction workers and professional chefs will tell you that quality blades don't matter. They do—quality craftsmanship matters.

It matters as much to the knifemakers as it does to collectors. Not only are makers of the world's finest knives pictured in this book conscientious enough to care about the quality of their work, but they also take pictures of the resulting blades, or have photographs taken, and write about them. Many of the feature articles in *KNIVES 2026* are written by renowned knifemakers and bladesmiths, such as Rick Dunkerley waxing poetic about "How Knife Shows Have Evolved," and Jason Fry penning "Today's Boomer Masters are Next Gen's Legends."

Non-maker authors have written articles covering "What's Trending in Knife Mechanisms," "MagnaCut Steel Cuts a Swath," "Tactical Fixed Blades Trend Hot," "Blue-Collar Splendor—the rise of replaceable blade technology and the utility knife," and "Half Century of Custom Knives." As has been the case for nearly half a century, the *KNIVES* annual feature articles are followed by "Trends," "State of the Art," and "Factory Trends" in handmade blades, and a complete Knifemakers Index.

Quality Craftsmanship. Think about that term for a moment, close your eyes, and picture all the handmade knives you've seen at shows, in display cases or retail cutlery cabinets, and within the pages of this book. And please, enjoy the immersive experience!

–Joe Kertzman

Wooden Sword AWARD

In a first for the "Wooden Sword Award," not only is this year's honor going to an antique piece, but also a sword. The story and photo are too good to pass up, and the owner of the sword happens to be an incredible art knife maker herself, so here we go (with credit going to *BLADE Magazine* Editor Steve Shackleford for the copy):

Scissors-making maven Grace Horne recently scored a find of a lifetime when she obtained the antique Scissor Sword made in 1851 by George Oates of Sheffield, England.

A Sheffield native, Grace thought she had lost out on the one-of-a-kind piece when someone else bought it after her computer crashed halfway through an auction of David Hayden-Wright's collection of historical British knives in 2023. However, a dealer contacted her in Spring 2024 with a picture of the piece, asking if she had ever seen it. Grace, of course, had seen the sword, asked who owned it, contacted the owner and bought it from him at the BLADE Show 2024.

Grace Horne

The sword was made especially for London's iconic 1851 Crystal Palace Exhibition and is in Wright's book *The Heritage of English Knives*. In part, Wright wrote the sword was "conceived to represent two completely different visual images, one an elegant diamond tapering blade flat-hilted court sword … the other an exceptionally large pair of attractive display tailor's scissors … The long, split blades form a diamond section with closing catch piece at the tip, each has foliated blued panels highlighted by the mirror polished steel, with the steel ribbed ricasso forming a concealed hinge.

"The split inner blade faces feature white frost-etched floral panels and the scrolled legend 'Manufactured by–George Oates–Sheffield.'"

"The bow knuckle guard and grip of solid nickel silver showcase piecrust edges surmounted by a large chased and engraved 'Monarch's crown.' The inner hilt supports fretted panels of raised foliate leaves and acorns with central scissor finger holes, the whole hilt being able to part and rejoin virtually invisibly." Respective blade and overall lengths: 31 and 36.8 inches.

We seriously doubt Grace and the Scissor Sword will part company anytime soon.

–Joe Kertzman

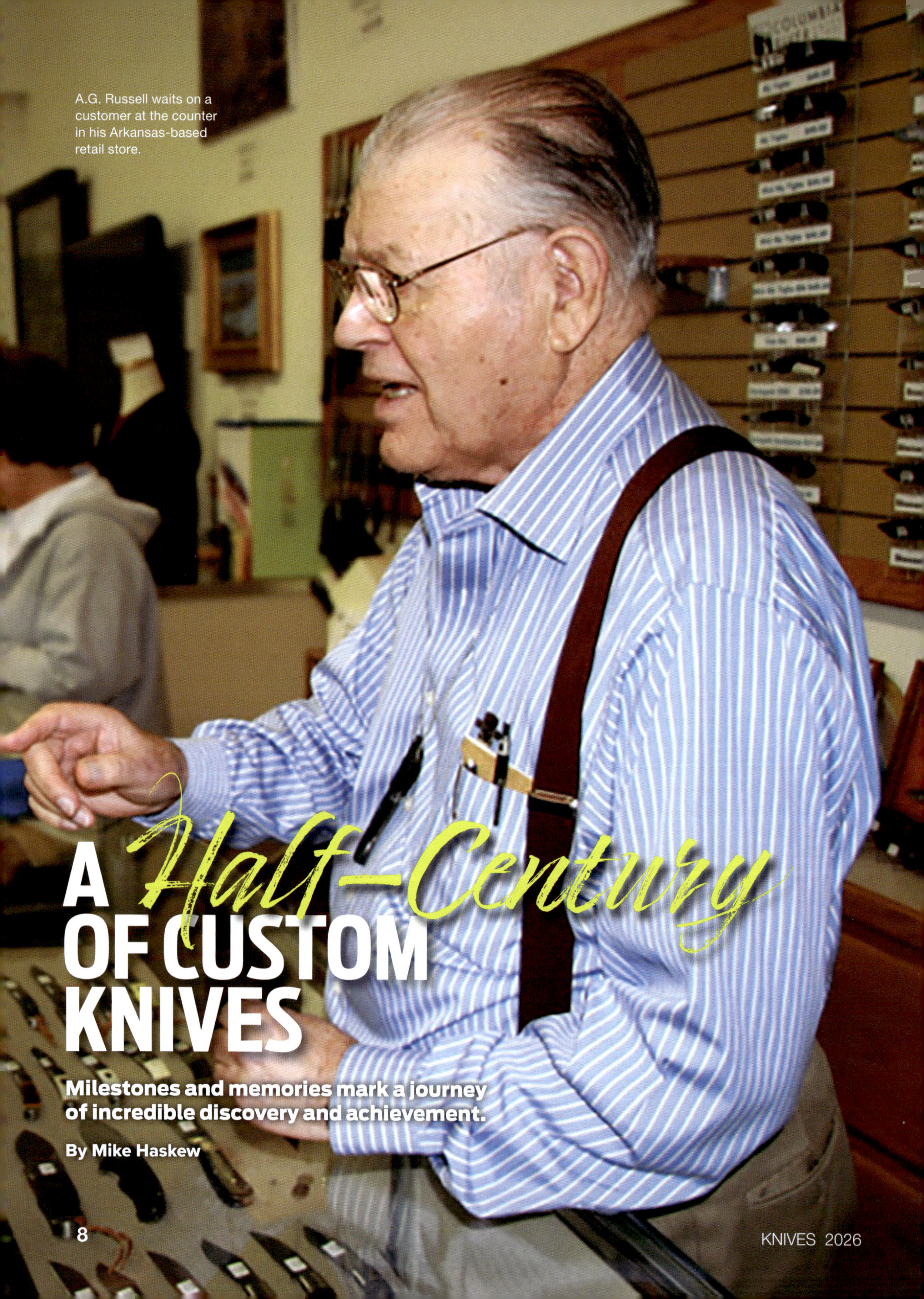

A.G. Russell waits on a customer at the counter in his Arkansas-based retail store.

A *Half-Century* OF CUSTOM KNIVES

Milestones and memories mark a journey of incredible discovery and achievement.

By Mike Haskew

For some, a half-century, give or take, is a lifetime. For others, such passing of time means a road long traveled. For the custom knife industry, the past 50 years have constituted a "golden age."

So much has been achieved. So many good people have come and gone. And more than a few moments that will be remembered forever have transpired. Since the 1970s, custom knifemaking has evolved, adapted, reinvigorated, and reached new heights in artistry and craftsmanship, while the appeal of the finished product has swept the breadth of the globe.

And it all seems to have happened so quickly. Time marches on, but it's fitting to take a moment and reflect on the past, our past, and in doing so, perhaps consider what is yet to come.

In the early 1970s, custom knifemaking was a somewhat shadowy endeavor. A table full of knives might be tucked away here and there in the corner of an immense hall at a gun show. Or an occasional classified ad for handmade knives might be in an outdoor magazine. All that changed when entrepreneur A.G. Russell was determined to bring custom knives to the forefront. And in time, multitudes took notice.

Russell was the catalyst for the first meeting of The Knifemakers' Guild in 1970, along with Bob Loveless, the Californian who became a legend in his own right. Russell bought tables and rented space for shows and helped makers to organize. In 1971, the first Guild Show was held in Houston, Texas, with about 20 knifemakers participating. A year later, the show was held in Kansas City, and the number of makers doubled. From there, it continued to climb.

"The founding of the Guild in 1971 is the watershed moment in custom knives," observes *BLADE Magazine* Editor and Cutlery Hall-of-Famer Steve Shackleford. "The contributions of the founding members led by A.G. Russell and Bob Loveless to establish a nationwide organization of custom knifemakers with an annual show, bylaws and more set the standard by which all other groups were judged.

"All the legendary makers—Bob Loveless, Bill Moran, Buster Warenski, George Herron, Ron Lake, Ted Dowell, Herman Schneider, Dan Dennehy, Michael Walker, Frank Centofante, Blackie Collins, Billy Mace Imel, Corbet Sigman, Jim Schmidt, Steve Schwarzer, Alfred Pendray, Bob Terzuola, Mel Pardue, Chris Reeve, Fred Carter, D' Holder, Jim Sornberger, to name but a few, belonged to the Guild at one time or another," Shackleford said.

Set the Standard

"The Guild Show was the first all-custom knife show and set the standard by which all other shows were judged," Shackleford says. "Having an organization with bylaws that protected both the maker and knife buyer was something that had never happened before, and the Guild showed the way. Knife enthusi-

From left to right, Billy Mace Imel, Carolyn Hughes, B.R. Hughes, Betty Dowell, and Steven Johnson smile for the camera at the 2015 Guild Show in the Muehlenbach Hotel of Kansas City.

Longtime knife purveyors Dan Delavan (left) and Neil Ostroff visit during a Guild Show.

asts, aficionados, and well-heeled collectors and knife buyers the world over attended, making it the first true international custom knife show as well."

Custom knifemaker Jim Sornberger remembers the early days of the Guild and its organization. "The Guild thing was first discussed in 1970, and that was Bob Loveless and A.G. Russell," Sornberger says. "Actually, A.G. bought tables for a bunch of the guys and set that up. He said, 'Let's have a show and get a block of tables,' and so he did that. The Guild was the best organization of knifemakers in the world, and it had the biggest knife show anywhere in the world for many years."

The late B.R. Hughes, a pioneer in cutlery journalism, the development of the American Bladesmith Society, and so much more, passed away in 2024. Before passing, he recalled those early days. "In the latter portion of the '60s, A.G. Russell, a dominant figure in the wonderful world of knives, supplied me with a list of all the custom makers he knew about at that time," Hughes related. "There were 21 names on the list. There are literally thousands of known makers in America today."

One reason for that surge in makers and markets was the Guild Show of 1973. It has become legendary for the reintroduction of damascus steel by the great Bill Moran. Hughes loved to tell the story of his arrival at that famous Guild event.

"This is one of my favorite subjects," he smiled. "Carolyn [Mrs. Hughes] and I drove to the Muehlebach Hotel in Kansas City for that Guild Show, and as we were pulling into the parking lot, a friend of mine came running out the door and said, 'Bill Moran's got eight damascus blades on his table!' And those were the hit of the show. I could hardly get the car parked fast enough to get inside and see them."

"I had no idea he was bringing damascus blades to the Guild Show until I got there," Hughes recalled. "It was a shock, and he sold several of them during the show. I think those eight knives saved bladesmithing. At the time, there were probably fewer than 15 bladesmiths in America, and the number was going down and not up. There had been Bo Randall and Rudy Ruana as well, but just a few younger bladesmiths."

Moran's damascus brought collector interest in the venerated steel, reenergizing its appeal to the masses. The rising tide lifted the entire custom knife industry. Indeed, by 1976, the American Bladesmith Society (ABS) was created by a dedicated group that included Moran and Hughes. Within two years, the ABS had opened its own school, and interest in the forged blade soared. Since then, the ABS has become the foremost organization for training, journeyman and master smith certification, and promotion of the forged blade in the world.

On Its Ear

"Moran's reintroduction of damascus steel for knife blades set the world of knives on its ear," Shackleford said. "People at that show in the Muehlebach Hotel of Kansas City went ape over the news that Moran had knives of damascus steel. The knives sold for $100-an-inch of blade steel at a time when $100 for a single custom knife was expensive.

"It helped set the stage for establishing custom knives as true collectibles that were worth a lot of money," he said. "Moran's reintroduction gave damascus, and forging in general, a needed shot in the arm, and bladesmiths everywhere started forging it. The reintroduction played a huge role in the rebirth of forging blades in America and set the stage for the creation by Moran, B.R. Hughes, Bill Bagwell, and Don Hastings of the ABS in 1976."

Centofante was a giant of the custom knife industry during an era of dramatic growth. His contribution to the Guild was immense. "Frank Centofante was one of the most influential custom knifemakers of his or any era," Shackleford said. "Under his leadership as Guild president, the Knifemakers' Guild enjoyed a golden era of shows in Orlando, Florida, in the 1990s, and a boom in outstanding knifemakers. A highlight was the 25th Anniversary Guild Show, where the organization's surviving members were honored, and comedian Shelley Berman gave a standup performance before an international audience of makers and collectors.

"Not only was Centofante a great leader, but he was one of the most popular knifemakers and personalities of his time. He made great knives but also made many friends through his engaging demeanor, great sense of humor, and willingness to help any and all Guild members in building their businesses."

Right in step with the growing interest in custom knives came reporting of the phenomenon. Loveless was the subject of a memorable *Sports Illustrated* article in 1980, and his long association with the introduction of the drop-point hunter, perhaps the most copied fixed-blade knife style in modern history, was soon brought to the forefront.

The wider custom knife industry, not just bladesmiths, but also stock-removal makers, gained momentum in the meantime, primarily due to the quality of the work, its increasing availability in quantity, and the accompanying publicity that steadily grew. Hughes and others had written a few knife articles through the years and occasionally got ink in a gun or outdoor publication. However, in 1973, custom knifemaker, inventor, and entrepreneur Blackie Collins founded *The American Blade*, the forerunner of today's *BLADE Magazine*. Along with other knife magazines that contributed, *The American Blade* was a trailblazer. And *BLADE Magazine*, having celebrated its 50th Anniversary three years ago, remains the world's number one publication of its kind.

"Beginning with its introduction by Blackie Collins in 1973 as *The American Blade* and continued through today as *BLADE,* the magazine has been a leader in promoting custom knives," Shackleford says. "From Sid Latham's story on the first Guild Show to those on Bill Moran's reintroduction of damascus, the boom in Michael Walker's LinerLock design, Jimmy Lile's Rambo knife, Buster Warenski's King Tut dagger, the BLADE Show, and much more, *BLADE* has always been on the leading edge of breaking stories on all the big custom knives and events. Long before social media, long before the Internet, long before the BLADE Show, *BLADE* was there to break all the big stories on custom knives and continues to do so to this day."

Collector Interest

With burgeoning collector interest in custom knives and more publicity, the number of shows increased steadily into the 1980s and '90s. The BLADE Show, California Custom Knife Show, New York Custom Knife Show, Art Knife Invitational and others opened to enthusiastic crowds. The work of some well-known makers became so popular that lotteries were instituted just for the chance to purchase one of their knives. An aftermarket boomed. Purveyors cultivated relationships with makers and buyers alike, and sales became brisk.

At the same time, Loveless was not only in high demand for his drop-point hunter but also brought attention to the most popular stainless steels of the period, 154CM and ATS-34. Russell remained a key player, too, with his extensive catalog business featuring a wide selection of knives and sharpeners, and his tireless advocacy of the industry.

Lake promoted the tab-lock interframe folder and

Far Left: Don Henderson (left) presents the W.W. Cronk Award to Ron Best at the 2007 Guild Show in Orlando, Florida.

Left: Edmund Davidson, a highly skilled maker of fully integral custom knives, holds his "Orgasmatron" creation on the floor of the Guild Show.

helped popularize 416 stainless as a viable blade steel. The Guild Show and other events presented prime opportunities for custom makers like Warenski, W.W. Cronk, Schmidt, and Virgil England to shine. One longtime maker said that this period "took us to another planet."

Buster Warenski's King Tut Dagger was a landmark creation in the history of custom knives and remains an iconic example of artistry in blades. (SharpByCoop photo)

In 1981, Walker debuted his famed LinerLock folder, adding a new dimension of titanium as a material two years later. That same year, Hollywood embraced Sylvester Stallone's Rambo knife from the film series of the same name. Two *BLADE Magazine* Cutlery Hall-of-Famers, Jimmy Lile and Gil Hibben, supplied the Rambo knives that became synonymous with adventure. The silver screen continued to bring custom knives into the mainstream with high-profile appearances in such films as the "Conan" series, "Commando," "Predator," and "The Last of the Mohicans."

Media interest is still a force today, and television programming like the "Forged in Fire" series, which premiered in 2015, has gained a loyal following.

Technology crept into the custom knifemaking equation in the 1990s with the advent of computer numerically controlled (CNC) equipment, CAD/CAM design, and laser-cutting capability. A debate surrounding the definition of a true handmade knife has ensued and persists to this day. Is it a requirement that every component be fashioned by hand, or is it reasonable to raise productivity by minimizing the monotonous, time-consuming elements of making a knife and refining finishes with the help of a machine? Everyone has their take on the topic.

Meanwhile, technology touched the custom knife community in other ways during the 1990s. The Internet and social media, as well as the resulting immediate communication, have broadened the marketability of the makers' work, and the global reach has opened doors for new entrants, both makers and collectors. Websites, forums, and how-to videos abounded, creating an unprecedented exchange of information and, of course, dollars. Still, most agree

B.R. Hughes (left) and Bill Moran attend an event with an anvil in the foreground, representative of their devotion to the forged blade. (Thomason photo courtesy of *BLADE Magazine)*

Above: David Darom (right) receives the Nate Posner Award from Wayne Hensley during the 2010 Guild Show.

Left: The legendary Bill Moran puts on a forging demonstration before a large audience. (Thomason photo courtesy of *BLADE Magazine)*

that buying based on images is quite a different experience from holding a knife in the hand and putting an eye directly on the knifemaker's best effort.

Through the years, trends have come and gone in custom knifemaking with varying degrees of staying power. The drop-point hunter will probably be around forever, and the tactical knife is a mainstay, while the fantasy genre, art knife, and the workaday camp, hunter and skinner will always be popular. Folding mechanics have been the focus of innovation and design creativity with Walker's LinerLock, the tail-lock system of Lake's interframe, Ken Onion's SpeedSafe one-handed opening system, or the bolt-action or trigger lock by Collins.

Fertile Ground

In all aspects of custom knifemaking, aesthetics, form, function, mechanics, materials, and ergonomics, the last half-century has provided fertile ground and countless opportunities to push the envelope. And from that adventurous spirit, collaborations between custom makers and factories have resulted in an unprecedented fusion of design and production prowess.

While it is impossible to include all the seismic and subtle changes that have occurred in the custom knife industry since the 1970s, no retrospective would be complete without mentioning just a few of the iconic knives and genres that have marked the last half-century. Along with Lake's interframe, Walker's Linerlock, Loveless's drop-point hunter and his Big Bear sub-hilt fighter, Moran's damascus, and other countless designs and materials, there are more memorable styles and individual pieces.

Ted Dowell brought the integral cap-and-hilt hunter to prominence. D.E. Henry's English Bowie set a standard of its own. Schmidt's goblin folders, Bob Lum's tanto blade configuration, and the near-flawless hunters of George Herron are unforgettable. Daryl Meier's American Spirit knife was presented to President George H.W. Bush in 1990, while Terzuola was busy earning the title of "Godfather of the tactical folder" with his ATCF. Tony Bose raised the slip joint folder to new heights, while Hibben produced dazzling fantasy pieces, and Wolfgang Loerchner rose to prominence in the art knife world.

Warenski, who began his knifemaking career in 1966 after seeing a photo of a knife made by Hibben, put the last touch on his famed King Tut Dagger in 1987. A special mention of that landmark moment in custom knife history is appropriate here. Buster's creation became famous worldwide, and Phil Lobred, who commissioned the breathtaking piece, once said, "I believe the King Tut Dagger is the greatest art knife made to date. It's so complex that it has not even been attempted by anyone else. It proved what could be achieved if the knifemaker was good enough and established a standard for the art of knifemaking."

As a reminder, the King Tut Dagger was finished with 32 ounces of gold, including the cast blade. It was the first of Warenski's famed "Legacy Knives" that also included the breathtaking Gem of the Orient, completed with 153 emeralds that weighed in at 10 karats, and nine diamonds at five karats, with gold filigree overlaying a jade handle. Fire and Ice completed the mesmerizing trilogy with 22 rubies, 75 diamonds, and 28 ounces of 18-karat gold.

Through the years, many personas, some larger than life, have made custom knifemaking what it is today, and Hughes will ever stand tall among them. "One of the four founders of the ABS, B.R. wrote about knives for almost 60 years," Shackleford says. "In addition to helping found the Society, B.R. served on its board of directors for 40 years. Not only was he an invaluable teacher and leader, but he also promoted the ABS and its members through many stories and profiles in all the major knife publications, not to mention his books on the subject. He was a one-man PR agency for the ABS for almost half a century. Along with Russell, B.R. was probably the most influential non-knifemaker in custom knife history."

At times, it seems like a half-century of custom knives has passed in the proverbial wink of an eye. But then, to look backward and consider the magnitude and meaning of many changes, the growth, potential realized, and dedication exhibited, the journey seems like a long road. In truth, it is a blend of the two, a perspective of past and present, and more exciting than anything else, a runway for future possibilities. □

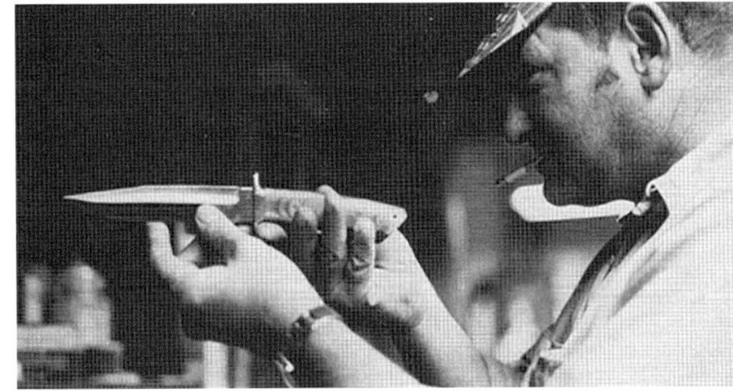

The legendary Bob Loveless checks the lines of a finished knife. Loveless remains a titan of the custom knife industry.

Knife Mechanisms: Gimmicks or *Game Changers?*

Folder features evolve at a fast clip as consumer demand drives innovation.

By Dave Rhea

Today's knife market is a dynamic mix of time-tested traditions, evolving design applications and cutting-edge innovations. Designs are as varied as the people who carry them, and what someone chooses as an everyday carry (EDC) knife can be a cultural marker as much as a cutting tool. One of the key features of EDC knives is their mechanical operation. In this article, we will explore the fascinating realm of folding knives, examining the influence of knife mechanisms on consumer preference, the evolution of some of the most iconic designs, and whether today's emerging ideas are gimmicks or game changers.

The folding knife industry is often associated with mechanical innovation. However, according to

Spyderco's Sage Series includes knives of the same basic design that highlight different lock mechanisms as homage to the history of their designers. The wheel of Sage models is arranged on binders of knife lock patents.

As its name suggests, the Spyderco Manix 2 Lightweight features ultra-lightweight construction and the Ball Bearing Lock mechanism, which can be seen in this custom cutaway version. The knife's overall length is 8 inches, with a 3.37-inch blade offered in multiple steel options, depending on the specific model.

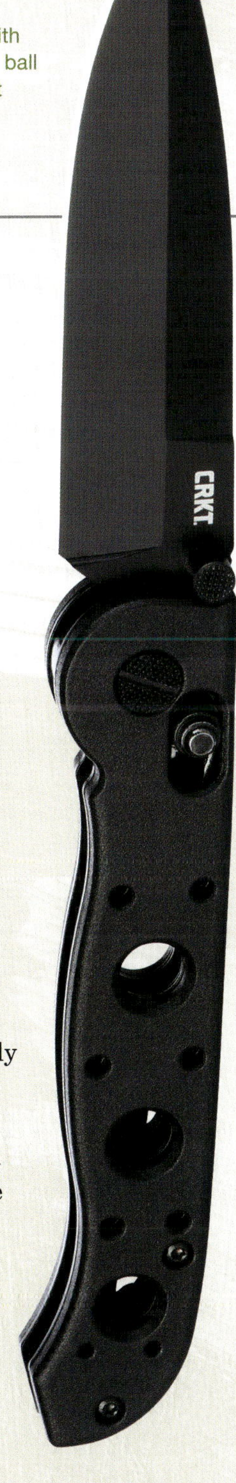

Part of the CRKT M16 series designed by Kit Carson, the M16-03XK features an ambidextrous Crossbar Lock paired with an IKBS (Ikoma Korth Bearing System) ball bearing pivot for seamless deployment and easy one-hand closing. It also has a lightweight Grivory aircraft-grade thermoplastic handle.

industry experts, there is a notable trend regarding classic slip-joint knives. The traditional non-locking folder, often affectionately called a pocketknife, is experiencing a demand revival.

"I'd go out on a limb and say that slip-joint knives are having a moment right now," said Doug Flagg, vice president of marketing and innovation at Columbia River Knife & Tool (CRKT). "Innovation will never go out of style, but in a lot of ways, what's old is new again." Flagg added that CRKT recognized this slip-joint revival and has already developed recent models to answer consumer demand, including the Symmetry and Venandi models, designed by Richard Rogers, and the Darriel Caston-designed, double-bladed Forebear.

Regarding specializing in traditional folders, W.R. Case & Sons is arguably second to none. On the topic of slip joints, Tony Difonzo, director of engineering at Case Knives, acknowledged that many people prefer the look and feel of tried-and-true knife designs, like Case's Sod Buster, Trapper and Stockman. He added that their less-intricate designs imply greater reliability.

"Sometimes, it's better to simplify and have something that you know is going to work repeatedly," Difonzo said. "The influence of debris and the wear and tear of repeated real-world use can cause a knife with complex components to not fire or lock up like it should. We don't want it to look cool on a shelf; we want it in people's pockets to use every day."

According to Difonzo, Case continues to meet their customers' demand for traditional knives by producing about 6,000 slip-joint knives daily, contrasting them with their locking knife line, which accounts for only about 20 percent of Case's overall consumer line.

Evolution of Modern Mechanisms

These days, many of the mechanisms we take for granted were once novel inventions conceived by imaginative innovators. For example, an assisted-opening knife didn't exist before Blackie Collins bringing his design to market, famously inspired by the single-strut suspension on his Ducati motorcycle. Before Michael Walker's revolutionary LinerLock design, closing a locked folding knife was virtually always a two-handed job. In subsequent years, variations and often improvements of both innovations began to proliferate in the industry and become all but ubiquitous. These are only two examples of numerous similar evolutions.

Time makes it easy for innovators who changed the industry to be forgotten

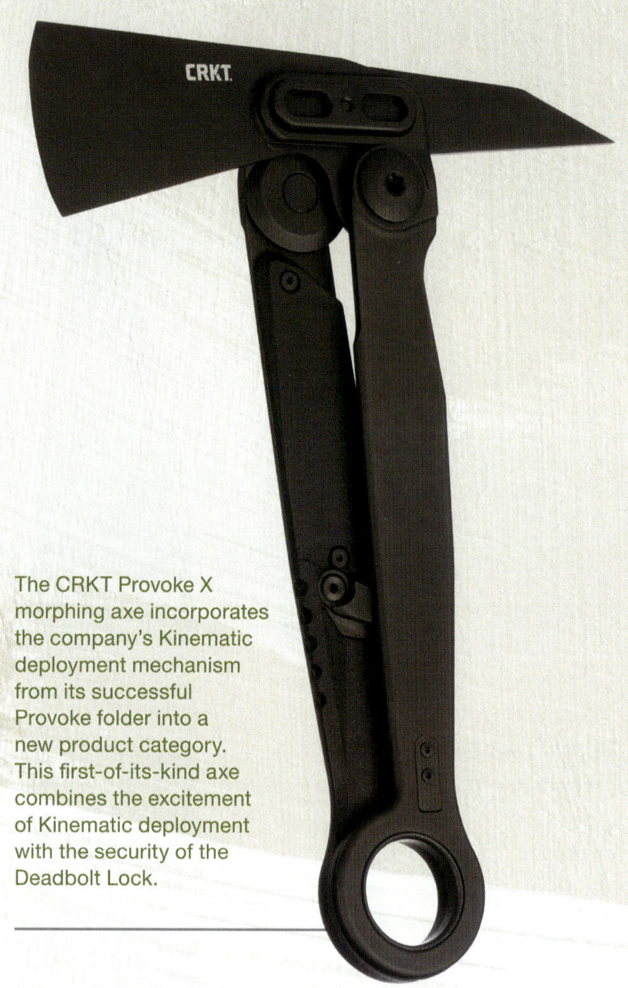

The CRKT Provoke X morphing axe incorporates the company's Kinematic deployment mechanism from its successful Provoke folder into a new product category. This first-of-its-kind axe combines the excitement of Kinematic deployment with the security of the Deadbolt Lock.

after expired patents, as their inventions become "democratized," as Michael Janich, special projects coordinator at Spyderco, characterized it. He drew careful attention to the importance of these noteworthy creation stories: "It's counterproductive when it comes to promoting industry education and a sense of history," Janich said. "People new to knives don't understand the origin of the mechanism or appreciate its history."

In 2008, Spyderco created the ongoing Sage Series to draw a historical line between pioneering locking mechanisms and the makers who created or popularized them to assign credit where credit is due. To accomplish this, each Sage Series model features a different key advancement. The Sage 1 incorporates two Michael Walker mechanisms: the LinerLock and the ball bearing detent. The Sage 2 features Chris Reeves' RIL (Reeve Integral Lock), a.k.a. the frame lock. Sage 3 features Blackie Collins' Bolt Action Lock, improved by Spyderco with easy-to-operate ambidextrous release buttons. Sage 4 pays tribute to Al Mar by integrating a mid-back lock, a signature element of Al Mar Knives. Completing the series, thus far, the Sage 5 and Sage 5 Lightweight models feature the Compression Lock designed by Spyderco Founder Sal Glesser.

Many folders included in Spyderco's current line-up feature the company's proprietary locks, such as the Para 3, a compact version of the popular Paramilitary 2 folder, featuring Glesser's Compression Lock, and the Manix 2 Lightweight, featuring a Ball Bearing Lock invented by Sal's son, Eric. Both locking mechanism patents have now expired.

Historical context intact or not, widespread adoption and adaptation of mechanisms due to patent expiration play a significant role in today's popular trends. Like any other patent, a knife mechanism patent expires after 20 years, after which the design enters the public domain. Then, anyone can legally manufacture and sell products incorporating that mechanism without requiring permission from the original patent holder. Along with Spyderco's recent expirations, the Benchmade Axis Lock patent also recently expired, which has been felt across the industry.

Versions of Their Own

"You'll note an uptick in knives featuring what was originally called the Axis Lock, now commonly referred to as the Crossbar Lock," Flagg said. "Now that it's available to the industry at large, many manufacturers, including CRKT, are coming to market with versions of their own."

CRKT began using the Crossbar Lock in 2024 and is now carrying it forward into the iconic Kit Carson-designed M16 collection. "It's got a fluidity and ease of use that consumers seem to gravitate towards, and I think you'll see more knives using the technology coming out each year," Flagg said.

Indeed, many other knife companies produce similar bar-style locks, often under different names, including Hogue's ABLE Lock, SOG's XR Lock, and Civivi's Superlock. Patent expiration also levels the playing field for smaller manufacturers by allowing them to use popular mechanisms without the cost or hassle of licensing, which is a game-changer.

Janich says that many of the hot new locks are subtle mechanical variations of the original Blackie Collins Bolt Action Lock from the 1970s, which, he added, never received the recognition it deserved. "The Bolt Action Lock was, to my knowledge, the first to be based on the mechanics of creating a ramp on

The Classic American Case Sodbuster Jr. is a testament to U.S. craftsmanship and durability. It embodies reliability, functionality, and traditional style all in a compact design. The Sod Buster Jr. in this photo has a 2.875-inch stonewashed skinner blade and a Smooth Black Canvas Laminate handle with Day Glow G10 liners.

the back of the blade and wedging a locking device between that ramp and the stop pin or backspacer."

As an in-line mechanism, he says, the wedge concept became the basis for the Axis Lock, Ball Bearing Lock, Arc Lock, and Stop Lock, and others, and it continues to be the basis for many of today's most popular locks, including the Shark Lock, Atlas Lock, and Superlock. "The in-house production secret is making the mechanics just different enough to convince the USPTO [United States Patent and Trademark Office] that it's unique."

Janich said he doesn't foresee any locks disappearing completely as new ones join the market. He mentioned that the classic back lock mechanism is still the bread and butter of many Spyderco designs. Though he acknowledges it's an old-school design, he attributes its continued popularity to seasoned knife users who, he said, tend to have strong preferences, especially when lock failure could result in bloodshed.

Gimmicks or Game Changers?

On one side of the demographics spectrum are seasoned knife users who field dress game and integrate EDC knives into their self-defense strategies. On the other side is the next generation of knife customers, whose industry knowledge mainly comes from YouTube influencers posting POV (point of view) knife reviews. The latter customer base is often mainly drawn to what is widely regarded as the "fidget factor," where interest and excitement are focused primarily on knives with intriguing opening, closing, and locking mechanisms. Smooth, snappy action is in demand, and the more intricate, the better. The sweet spot, one might tease, is somewhere between steampunk design and a Rube Goldberg machine.

"There are lots of younger knife users who have never had to use a knife hard," Janich said. "In many cases, they like fidget-friendly designs that open and close easily and are entertaining."

Bryan Winters, owner of Winterblade Knives and a relative newcomer to the knife industry, doesn't have concerns about "fidget factor" characterizations, despite his knives being on the cutting edge of fidgetry. He captures his philosophy by saying, "We can't spell function without fun." Winters started making his earliest creations in his modest shop in 2019, but 2022 was the year he launched his flagship design, the Factor, a stout, legitimately dependable

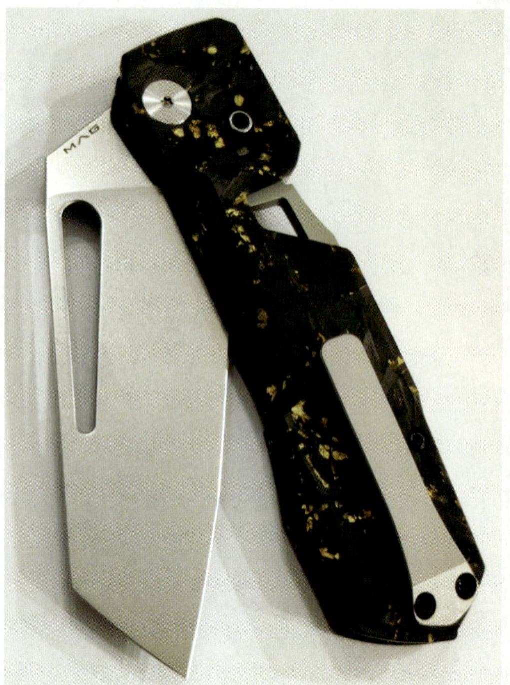

Winterblade's Factor 8ight features an all-new "QUAD Magnet Detent System," the company's strongest and most adjustable magnetic detent system to date, as well as an updated "M-Lock Plus" magnet-driven blade lock, and improved titanium flip-lever deployment mechanism for snappy action.

folder, featuring cutting-edge new mechanisms that integrate magnets into the locking and deployment systems.

"I've never set out to design a knife just because I think it will sell well or because it's a certain gimmick," Winters said. "I'll use magnets, but if I think springs are better suited for that particular mechanism, I'll use springs, or maybe I'll need some sort of lever or gears, whatever the case may be."

He explained that, in the Factor, and later incarnations like the Factor 8ight, the detent magnets "suck the blade in" and keep it securely closed. An added benefit is alleviating the contact point of friction with a typical detent ball, allowing for noticeably smoother deployment. A benefit of the neodymium magnets is that they retain their power for almost a century, whereas springs fatigue or wear out much more quickly through continued use.

"My point with the people who say that magnets are gimmicks is, you can do things with magnets, physically speaking, that you cannot do with springs."

One of his imaginative non-magnetic locking mechanisms is the Stealth Lock, as featured on his Severn model. "It's kind of like an Axis Lock and Shark Lock hybrid, but it was designed from the ground up," he said, emphasizing that the Stealth Lock is not an evolution of either existing design. It features crossbar-like studs in the handle scales on both sides and a fin-like forefinger latch that retracts into the hilt, eliminating the protrusion of the Shark Lock. Interestingly, the mechanism has a single compression spring that performs "dual actuation," as Winters put it. In other words, the same spring that loads the lock also loads the latch.

Radical Reimagination

Another novel Winters creation is his radical reimagination of a double-action firing mechanism on the Darkfire OTF. Instead of a typical fixed slider, the blade is propelled in and out via a large blade guard that acts as a lever. The stylized blade guard is part of an overall design aesthetic inspired by the Mandalorian Darksaber from "Star Wars." Inside, the brilliantly reimagined, simplified mechanism is powered by a single compression spring, again departing from traditional designs.

Regarding the "fidget factor," Winterblade knives are a fidget paradise. They are a new and radically different experience. The folders are outlandishly pleasing to repeatedly open and close. The speed and weight are on target, and the lock-up on each is tight and satisfying. Even the sound is different. Whether it's a seemingly magical magnetic lock, Darkfire OTF's simplified single-spring action, or the ultra-complex double-action, side-opening automatic Greywalker model (yet to be released as of writing this article), it's easy to see that the fidget-factor runs unencumbered throughout his designs. However, upon closer examination, it's just as easy to realize that Winters' creative passion and technical curiosity motivate him to break fresh ground in the fertile field of knife mechanism innovation.

"I see a lot of variation in the knife industry as far as materials and profiles, but I don't see a whole ton of variation in the mechanics of the knives," Winters said. "And that's exactly what I enjoy doing—the mechanical side of things."

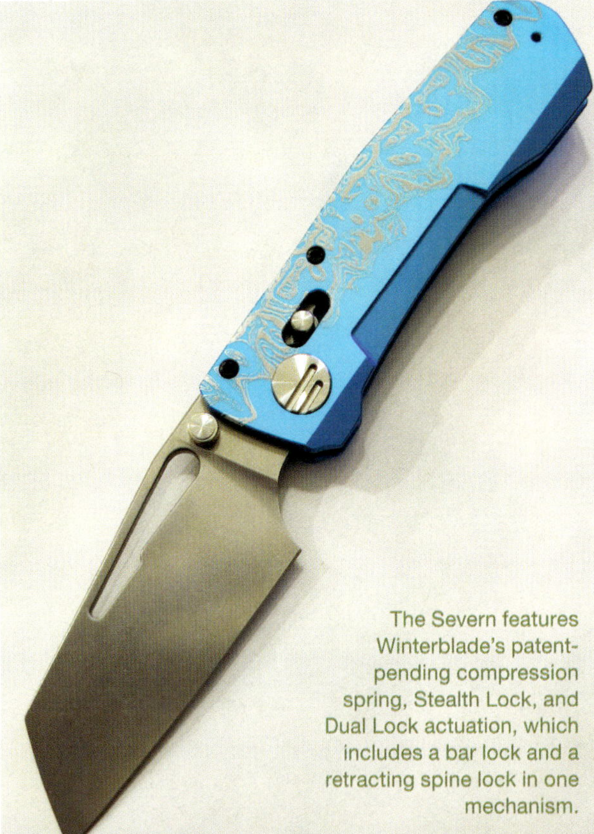

The Severn features Winterblade's patent-pending compression spring, Stealth Lock, and Dual Lock actuation, which includes a bar lock and a retracting spine lock in one mechanism.

Whether one prefers the simplicity of a traditional slip joint, the fidget-friendly nature of modern deployment and locking systems, or the cutting-edge ingenuity of truly novel mechanisms, one requirement for success is that function meets the real-world needs of end users. Examples that Flagg pointed out in the current CRKT line are Flavio Ikoma's proprietary Deadbolt Lock design, featured on several of the company's knives since its creation five years ago, and Joe Caswell's Kinematic opening system, which Flagg characterized as "a true innovation marker." The Kinematic mechanism has several pivot points and linkage arms that "morph" into the opened knife when manually actuated.

"Joe is a bit of a mad scientist, in the best sense of that term, and his Provoke knife, with its Kinematic opening technology, was an instant best seller for us," Flagg says of its 2019 release. "Now, we've taken it to the next level and brought this innovation into our Provoke X, a morphing tactical axe that combines Kinematic opening with the Deadbolt Lock to create an EDC axe unlike anything the industry has seen before."

Conversely, Flagg pointed out that sometimes manufacturers mistakenly think they are onto something, but customers ultimately show them the way. "For example, we thought our Ken Onion Field Strip mechanism would be a game changer in the industry, but we didn't see the pick-up we thought we would. In the end, it seems that not enough people are worried about cleaning their knives in the field without any tools, so we're moving on to other, more relevant technologies."

The knife industry has a long legacy of benefiting from an enduring heritage while enabling innovators to push boundaries. It engages a wide variety of collectors and enthusiasts by offering as many knife designs as there are preferences and needs, whether nostalgic, futuristic or anywhere in between. Today's trends show no indication of that dynamic subsiding in the foreseeable future. As such, all indicators point to an industry that will remain both reassuring and exciting. □

The Benchmade 593BK-01 P.S.K., featuring a 3.4-inch drop-point MagnaCut blade in a black Cerakote finish, is the company's foray into a heavy-duty folder built to withstand the rigors of an outdoor environment. The blade shape and handle design work together to build user confidence.

MagnaCut Steel Cuts a Wide Swath

Dr. Larrin Thomas describes what led to his development of the modern alloy.

By Dexter Ewing • Marty Stanfield images

Knife enthusiasts jump at the chance to try out anything new—blade locks, materials, designs, brands and steels satisfy their cravings. Steel especially. When you look at all the advanced high-tech alloys currently on the market, at one point in time, they were brand new, and with the introduction of each, there was a certain amount of frenzy and hype. One thing is certain: the industry loves high performance, so getting blades fashioned from the latest steels into the hands of those who will use them is the end goal.

You've noticed a leapfrogging trend if you've been on the knife scene for a while. Common catchphrases include "the bigger the better," "stays sharp longer," "holds an edge better," and so forth. The relatively new high-performance blade steel, CPM MagnaCut, or MagnaCut for short, has taken the knife industry by storm, leapfrogging the competition in today's market. Shortly after its official release, manufacturers began offering some of their existing models in it. Blades made from MagnaCut sold fast.

Crucible Industries, LLC, a leader in powder metallurgy technology and producer of MagnaCut, has been busy over the decades introducing high-tech blade steels to the industry, such as 154CM, CPM 154, S30V, S35VN, S45VN, S60V and S90V. The company has a track record of creating modern alloys used in high-end factory knives with blades known for their superior edge holding capabilities and toughness. In a sense, MagnaCut is leapfrogging others as a cutting-edge blade steel with all the properties hardcore knife users want in an alloy.

MagnaCut is celebrated for its unprecedented

Designed by custom knifemaker Richard Rogers, the limited edition "Q" from CRKT is an upscale everyday carry folder featuring a titanium handle, carbon-fiber inlays, and a MagnaCut blade.

balance of toughness, corrosion resistance, and edge holding, incorporating 10.7% chromium into the steel makeup, 1.15% carbon, 2% each of vanadium and molybdenum and .3% niobium carbides. MagnaCut boasts the same performance characteristics as CPM 4V tool steel, which does not have the new steel's stain- or corrosion-resistant properties.

Metallurgist Dr. Larrin Thomas, no stranger to the knife industry, developed MagnaCut. Many know Larrin's father, *BLADE Magazine* Cutlery Hall of Famer Devin Thomas, a modern-day pioneer in the forging of damascus and a stalwart of the knife industry. When the younger Thomas was a teenager, his father took him to knife shows, kindling his interest in blade metallurgy.

"Because my favorite aspect of knives was the metallurgy of steel, I read as much as I could, like Dr. John Verhoeven's book on steel metallurgy he wrote for bladesmiths," Thomas says. "I would also ask all my questions about steel to metallurgists from Crucible Steel at knife shows and on phone calls."

Thomas took it upon himself to email Dr. Verhoeven and ask for his advice on what is involved in becoming a metallurgist. Verhoeven told Thomas that he would need to be good at math, advice he took to heart, enrolling in a junior college and working with a math professor who groomed his curiosity and instilled confidence in him to pursue a material engineering degree.

"I don't think there are too many people with a Ph.D. in engineering who started with pre-calculus at a two-year university," Thomas said.

One of his early interests in metallurgy was the process of developing a blade steel. "S30V was released around the time I developed an interest in steel, and I wanted to learn everything I could about how Crucible decided how much of this element and that element should go into the alloy," he said.

The Emerson Knives Com Seven is a marriage of two popular designs—the sinewy recurved blade of the company's Commander model, but in MagnaCut steel, and the no-nonsense handle design of the CQC-7.

Steel in His Veins

Currently, Thomas is employed in research and development for the United States Steel Corporation (U.S. Steel) located in the greater Pittsburgh area. His specialty is the development of new automotive sheet steels, finding the harmonic balance between strength and ductility, and making alloys that are stronger yet easy to work with from a manufacturing standpoint. So, pretty much his whole life has revolved around steel.

The KnifeCenter Exclusive Hogue K320 takes the standard K320 folder and elevates it to new levels with a 3-D machined aluminum handle and a MagnaCut blade. This configuration is only available from KnifeCenter (knifecenter.com).

What exactly inspired him to create MagnaCut? A few years after he embarked on a career with U.S. Steel, Thomas started "Knife Steel Nerds," an online blog about steel and the heat treatment thereof, which was aimed at knifemakers and knife consumers. The blog allowed him to deeply compare available blade steels and how heat treatment variables affected each alloy's performance.

"I found there was a divide between the best non-stainless powder metallurgy steels and the best stainless powder metallurgy steels," he says.

For example, Thomas says non-stainless CPM 4V has a higher toughness than stainless CPM S30V, despite the two having similar wear resistance. "I thought there was a way to give stainless steels a similar microstructure to the non-stainless steels and thus match the properties while still being corrosion resistant."

Thus began his search for a new knife steel to bridge the gap. "This was done by reducing the chromium content and then keeping the carbon content in a relatively narrow window where the hardness is still high after heat treating," he said, "but it doesn't form the soft chromium carbides that make the properties of stainless steels worse. Despite the reduced chromium content, corrosion resistance is better than with most other stainless knife steels because of that same reduction of chromium carbides."

And with that, CPM MagnaCut was officially conceived.

Thomas also conducted his own tests on MagnaCut. He tested nearly every steel used to make knives through his work on Knife Steel Nerds. "So, when I got [MagnaCut] steel from the first batch, I started with my series of tests right away," he said. "Every positive result provided some relief along with more apprehension that it might fall down in the next test."

He first measured basic heat treating and hardness, pleasantly discovering that MagnaCut achieved a target Rockwell hardness of 60-64 RC. "The big surprise was that corrosion resistance was so good when I had expected it to be more in line with S30V and S35VN. Reducing the chromium carbide content to near-zero had a bigger effect than I expected."

What are the major selling points of CPM MagnaCut steel? "The primary selling point is the superior

The iconic Kabar USMC fighting knife is one of the most recognizable military models, but Spartan Blades breathed new life into the design by using MagnaCut blade steel. Old school design and new materials help introduce the legendary USMC fighting knife to a new generation.

balance of properties to prior stainless blade steels. For its level of wear resistance, in the same range as S30V or S35VN, it has greatly improved toughness," Thomas said.

Improved Edge Retention

He explained that better edge retention is possible if the knifemaker or manufacturer gives the blade a thinner cutting edge for improved cutting performance. "MagnaCut has improved corrosion resistance compared to popular stainless blade steels like S30V, S35VN, and M390," he said. "Spyderco has even been using it in their Salt Series knives, known for excellent resistance to rusting in saltwater conditions."

From a custom knifemaker or manufacturer standpoint, what are some of the things that one needs to be aware of when working with MagnaCut? Thomas states that some custom knifemakers have become accustomed to steels with low wear resistance, and thus they don't like performing a hand-rubbed satin finish on MagnaCut, something that has been an issue for years with other vanadium-alloyed steels like S30V. "In terms of grindability, it is a bit better than S30V, but it still wouldn't match the ease of steels like 1095 or 52100 with their soft carbides and much lower wear resistance."

According to Thomas, MagnaCut was released when knife consumers requested blades with higher Rockwell hardness properties. "Some manufacturers have had teething pains from making that transition," he says.

However, he is flattered to see his steel now used for so many blades across the board in the knife industry. "It has definitely been gratifying to see MagnaCut used in so many knives, and by some of my favorite knifemakers and manufacturers," he says.

Thomas is also amazed that the buzz and hype for MagnaCut has developed a life of its own. "I established credibility in the preceding years by writing my Knife Steel Nerds blog and the book *Knife Engineering*," he said. "But ultimately the buzz for the steel took on a life of its own and I no longer have much effect on it."

At this point, most manufacturers and some custom knifemakers are using MagnaCut. If you can try out MagnaCut for yourself, give it a whirl. You might find it to your liking with the optimum balance of wear and corrosion resistance never seen in any high-performance blade steel on the market.

I have carefully selected a few knives with MagnaCut blades to feature herein. Just keep in mind that there are many more MagnaCut models available than those showcased.

The Emerson Knives Com Seven is an interesting hybrid that combines the best design elements from two of Emerson's best-selling models into one exciting knife. Taking the sexy recurved clip-point blade of the Emerson Commander and mating it with the handle of the CQC7, the Com Seven was born. The hybrid model sports a 3.3-inch MagnaCut scaled-down Commander blade with a signature recurved edge, a long swedge grind, and a notched thumb ramp for extra control. The curved handle seemingly fits any size grip and remains comfortable for extended use. Dual titanium liners provide a solid backbone, and the LinerLock solidly engages and is easily released by pushing the exposed lock bar with the thumb. Textured G-10 handle scales provide ample traction for the ultimate non-slip grip.

Diamond Sharpening Rods

Recurved blades are great at slicing due to the blade belly followed by an inside curve to catch rope or other media in a slashing or pulling motion. It takes a different sharpening method to hone a recurved blade, however, than a straight- or standard curved-edge blade. Diamond sharpening rods are useful in following the edge of a recurved blade.

With their enhanced ergonomics and effective blade shapes, Emerson Knives are made to be used, and the slicing power of the Com Seven should be experienced firsthand. The manufacturer's suggested retail price (MSRP) is $295. The Com Seven is made in the USA and available in a black or satin-finished blade.

The Sig Sauer K320 tactical folder, made by Hogue Knives, is meant to be a counterpart to the Sig P320 pistol. The K320 is a brawny folder that would make a great backup tool for law enforcement or aware citizens. It features Hogue's ABLE Lock crossbar housed in an ergonomic handle that feels as good as it looks. The K320 comes with a choice of a clip-point or tanto MagnaCut blade for ultimate versatility.

Hogue dealer KnifeCenter of the Internet (KCI) offers an exclusive edition of the K320 on its website (knifecenter.com). Available in a stonewashed clip-point or tanto MagnaCut blade, the KCI Exclusive K320 features a black hard-anodized aluminum handle in exclusive 3-D machine patterning. The aggressive profile of the tanto blade (showcased in this article) pairs well with the handle. A deep carry pocket clip has four-way mounting capabilities, allowing for left- or right-hand as well as tip-up or tip-down carry. The KnifeCenter Exclusive K320 is a solid tactical folder made in the USA. The MSRP: $179.95.

Perhaps the most famous fixed-blade fighter used by the U.S. armed forces, the Kabar USMC fighting knife, has been carried in many theaters of war, serving well as a weapon and cutting tool. Its signature 7-inch clip-point blade features a pronounced swedge and fuller complemented by a non-slip stacked leather washer handle, and a heavy-duty buttcap that allows the knife to be used as an expedient hammer in a pinch.

Spartan Blades offers an advanced, high-end version of the Kabar USMC fighting knife. The same dimensions as the original, it showcases a MagnaCut blade in a choice of black or Flat Dark Earth (tan/brown) PVD coating, and a molded Kraton G handle that's impervious to weather and offers an excellent nonslip grip and good impact resistance. True to the original, the Spartan Blades Kabar elevates a legendary knife to iconic levels. Large grooves in the round, comfortable handle quickly displace water, and there's enough blade tip for detailed cutting.

Unlike the double-guard Kabar USMC fighter, the Spartan Blades version sports a single guard. Curtis Iovito, co-owner and founder of Spartan Blades, says the single guard makes it easier for a knife user to place their thumb on the blade spine to choke up for more control on the large knife. Available in a leather or molded Kydex sheath from Chattanooga Leather Works, the fit is purposely snug, requiring a bit of pull to extract the blade from the sheath so the knife does not accidentally jar loose while carrying it. Two straps on the sheath are compatible with any MOLLE attachment, or the knife can be toted via standard belt carry. The Spartan Kabar has an MSRP of $385 and is made in the USA.

The Benchmade 593BK-01 P.S.K. Axis Lock folder is the latest in the company lineup to showcase a MagnaCut blade. At 3.4 inches long, the drop-point blade has a black Cerakote coating and dual red ambidextrous thumb studs as a visual pop. Excelling at food prep and bushcraft or camp utility chores, outdoors is where the corrosion-resistant MagnaCut steel shines. The edge has good bite and can handle whittling and making fire starter fuzz sticks, and the choil area of the blade is designed for striking a ferrocerium rod to spark a campfire. The ergonomic black G-10 handle scales and carbon-fiber bolster are 3-D machined in large grooves for hand traction and distinct aesthetics. The P.S.K. is toted tip-up via a deep carry pocket clip, while the blade is secured open by the famous Axis Lock mechanism. The P.S.K. is also assisted opening for rapid blade deployment. There are so many features packed into this knife that it's nothing short of astounding. The Benchmade 593BK-01 P.S.K. is made in the USA and carries an MSRP of $450. □

Spyderco has been a heavy adopter of MagnaCut's excellent edge retention and corrosion resistance properties, finding a home for the steel in the Salt Series of knives, including Para 2 and Para 3 Salt models.

Tactical Fixed Blades Trend Hot

The choice is yours on blade style, steel, balance and handle ergonomics.

By Les Robertson • Photos by Robertson's Custom Cutlery

The custom knife market is divided. In one half are folders, and in the other, fixed blades. We have all witnessed the market share move from folders to fixed blades and back again. The three main reasons for the fluctuation are: something new becoming popular, saturation of a sector, and pricing. The custom knife buyers will sort all that out.

Popularity can be impacted by something as simple as a new steel, handle material or a knife gadget that is more challenging to design and build, such as a blade lock or opener. Popular market categories inspire experienced and new makers to build that type of knife. Two problems arise from this: 1) Makers will rapidly join a popular market category, but collectors are slower to follow. This has the unwanted effect of creating more supply, while not creating more demand; and 2) The pricing of the new makers' work in this category is primarily based on what other makers are getting for their work at that time, instead of, for example, the quality of their work, name recognition, and status among their competition.

Higher prices from less-qualified makers encourage well-known knifemakers to raise their prices, and the cycle continues until the knives become unaffordable. At this point, the collector will look for a new type or category of custom knife to buy. Which market sector will get the attention of those looking beyond the overpriced and/or saturated market? Tactical knives.

Because I am a custom knife dealer, I watch the market closely. Part of my job is to identify movement in market sectors, not only innovative types of handmade knives, but also skilled makers, new materials, or anything else that will cause a collector to take a second look.

One custom knife category has been referred to by various names over the years—combat, military, fighting, and most recently, tactical knives. I bought my first one in 1984. I didn't even know it was a tactical knife. Like most market sectors, the tactical fixed blade market never completely disappears. Over the years, fixed blade popularity has waned, then ebbed and flowed, but the sector has never disappeared. In 2025, we saw a renewed interest in tactical fixed blades. This increased demand will continue into 2026, primarily due to three reasons: diversity of styles in the tactical fixed blade arena, diversity of materials and price point.

Diversity of Styles

The word "tactical" is a marketing term that first appeared in the knife industry in 1995. It referred more to the look of a knife than its style or function. In 2000, I was asked by the owner of the BLADE Show to define parameters for a tactical folder and fixed blade when it came to knife judging. My definition was straightforward. There were no style, length, or material parameters, with a few exceptions. The blades and guard/bolster material (if there was a guard or bolster) of a tactical knife had to have non-reflective finishes, and the handle material must be synthetic, not natural. You would not believe the grief I have gotten over this simple definition.

With the definition in mind, there were no restrictions on blade length and grind; the utilization of a single or double edge; a single or double guard; integral guard, or lack of guard altogether; or the subsequent build of a knife. The only parameter for handle material was that it be synthetic, and non-reflective finishes could range from machine satin to bead blast, a tumble finish, black phosphate, or commercial finishes such as Gun-Kote and Cerakote. Commercial finishes upped the ante, being available in colors like black and green.

The resulting variety of custom tactical knives entered in competition was mind-blowing once this became a judging category. I was amazed, too, at the new styles and materials incorporated into knives I judged in other competitions or saw on tables at knife shows.

Diversity of Materials

Regarding tactical fixed blade materials, we are primarily talking about blade steel and hardware. Because many early tactical knives, as is the case today, were being used daily, the pros and cons of traditional steels such as 440C, ATS-34, and D-2 began to be examined. Consequently, new steels not generally associated with knives gained interest. Tactical fixed blades and folders introduced an explosion of steel to the custom knife market, such as CPM 3V, S35VN, S60V, and S90V, and powdered steel variants of traditional and new steels.

Additionally, custom knifemakers tried materials like Stellite, Talonite, and even ceramics for knife blades. Most of these were introduced to the custom knife world through tactical knives.

The initial choices for tactical knife handle material were limited to synthetics such as G-10, Micarta, and 550 Paracord. However, the options expanded rapidly with the introduction of G-11, carbon fiber, "Lightning Strike" carbon fiber, copper carbon fiber, Carbo Quartz, FatCarbon, antique Micarta, and others.

Price Point

The price of a custom knife has been a significant consideration over the last several years. For many collectors, price point has given them pause to reconsider not only what value range is the best fit for their collection, but also to better understand each knifemaker's position in the market. Is that maker charging the appropriate price for their work and position in their market? To that end, tactical fixed blades are more fundamental than many counterparts in the art knife, presentation and damascus categories.

Tomasz Dziubinski's "Nomad" camp knife enlists a 10-inch Sleipner stainless steel blade in a black Cerakote finish, an OD green G-10 handle and a Kydex sheath.

Another critical factor is heat-treating, which is manipulating the steel's mechanical properties, such as hardness, tensile strength, shock resistance, and corrosion resistance, among others. Proper heat treatment improves machinability and reduces brittleness.

Blade tempering is done after the steel has been hardened. Through tempering, a blade is reheated at a lower temperature than that used to heat treat it, allowing stresses in the blade to dissipate while maintaining the desired hardness. Each type of steel has different requirements for hardening and tempering. Learning about a particular steel's composition, Rockwell hardness, heat treatment, and tempering goes a long way in finding the correct alloy for the tasks a user or collector requires from their custom tactical fixed blade.

Because many of these knives will be used, the Latin phrase *caveat emptor* (let the buyer beware) is particularly applicable to the custom tactical knife market sector. Hype is very pervasive in this market. Individual research is recommended for the user/collector. Do not rely on the thousands of Internet

The Piotr Gosciniak "Tracker" model benefits from a black Cerakote-finished Sleipner stainless steel blade, a black textured G-10 handle, and the maker's own Kydex sheath.

Cost considerations for natural handle materials, exotic blade steel, and embellishments like engraving or scrimshaw are not as much of a concern when purchasing tactical fixed blades. Additional time (and cost) associated with labor-intensive knifemaking steps like forging damascus or working ivory (which is very slow work) are considerations for collectors and will continue to be so in 2026.

Due to the diversity of designs and styles, tactical fixed blades offer the collector numerous choices in that sweet spot of $400-$900, which is within many custom knife buyers' budgets.

Right Tool for the Job

It is the responsibility of knife collectors, as it is the makers, to do their homework about what cutting tasks different steels will and won't perform. Rockwell hardness and heat treating come into play, as tactical fixed blades are designed and built for use. The Rockwell hardness test tells a knife user how quickly a certain steel will dull. A Rockwell hardness of 52-54 RC is the minimum hardness for a utility or using knife. Most premium steels are in the 58-60 RC range.

The "Vanguard Cheetah Sub-Hilt Fighter" by Phillip Patton sports an 8-inch, satin-finished W-2 blade, a stainless guard with an indexing radius cutout, black Micarta handle and Micarta and stainless spacers.

Rafal Kolakowski's "Vanguard Ridgeline" model can be used for many tasks in the field. It combines the quality of being lightweight with durable materials and excellent handle ergonomics.

commandos and experts for your information.

Experienced and entry-level makers alike build tactical fixed blades that feature a blade and two pieces of handle material. Utilitarian design elements that give such knives a more tactically cool look will often add nothing of value. Frequently, design elements such as holes in the blades or handles, cutouts, and serrations will take away from the structural integrity of the knife. Usually, this fantasy look is done purely to catch the buyer's eye.

Regarding tactical fixed blades, be cautious about integral guards. Such knives are often laser cut or machined using a CNC machine, with the guards being small, exposed and jutting out at right angles. The squared-off edges are almost always sharp and will, as I unfortunately can attest, cut the skin between a user's thumb and forefinger. Combined with two pieces of handle material, integral-guard fixed blades are a quick and inexpensive build. I don't mind the idea of the integral guard, but I always insist that the maker cover it with the handle material, allowing the sharp edges to be rounded and the guard to be contoured to fit the user's hand.

Did You Win?

Over 25 years of standing behind countless tables at knife shows, I have witnessed several knife fights at each show. Let me clarify that: imaginary knife fights. Buyers see a particular knife (usually a large tactical fixed blade or bowie), pick it up, and swing it around in a way that looks like they're engaged with an imaginary opponent. When they stop and we make eye contact, I always ask, "Did you win?" Without exception, they smile with an odd combination of embarrassment and satisfaction.

As with most knife buyers, their initial attraction to a knife is visual. The desired look, lines, and materials may differ for each person, but the visual

Dave Broadwell's limited edition "Vanguard Guardian" is highlighted by its integral titanium guard and sub-hilt. The knife also has a blade fuller, or blood groove. It comes with a Nita Broadwell custom leather sheath.

A matching pair of Rafal Kolakowski "Spectra" daggers has a determinedly military look and feel, here in black Cerakote-finished Becut steel blades, black carbon-fiber handles and custom Kydex sheaths. (Rafal Kolakowski photo)

Michal Komorovsky offers his "Vanguard Paladin II" in an 8-inch, DLC-coated Elmax steel blade, stainless guard, and black Micarta handle with stainless spacers and a thong hole. For it, the maker fashioned a leather sheath.

experience draws them to the knife. Most makers of tactical fixed blades try to integrate the desired cutting tasks and the knives' intended uses into their designs. They also do their best to integrate both handle ergonomics and balance to make each knife comfortable.

The issue for small utility knives, hunters, and folders is the blade-to-handle ratio. Arguably, the most comfortable knife handle size is 4.75-5.5 inches in length. Handles this long would look odd on hunters and folders. In the case of folding knives, it would make them uncomfortable to carry, defeating one of the primary purposes of a folder. A knife that is uncomfortable to carry or not balanced is often also visually unappealing.

Once a knife catches your eye, you impulsively want to handle it. For many, this is where the magic happens. A visceral reaction occurs when you put the knife in your hand. The proper symmetry, balance, and handle ergonomics instantly allow the knife to become an extension of the user, making it effortless to use.

Phillip Patton's "Vanguard Intrepid" boasts a 7-inch, satin-finished AEB-L blade, a stainless guard and sub-hilt and a black Micarta handle. It comes with a leather sheath from the maker.

Because custom tactical fixed blades are built for use, this becomes a driving force in incorporating design elements for the knives' intended purposes, as well as the materials chosen for blades, guards and handle materials. This is an area where tactical fixed blades excel. Because of the variety of styles and materials, you can easily match up a tactical knife to meet your needs, be that a large fixed-blade tactical or a small utility knife for camping, bushcraft work or even an EDC.

Some Favorite Custom Knives

A knife like Rafal Kolakowski's "Vanguard Ridgeline" model can be used for many tasks in the field. It combines the quality of being lightweight with durable materials and excellent handle ergonomics.

At the other end of the spectrum are big choppers. The large, heavy blades are designed to do what small knives can't—break a trail, create firewood, and assist in processing large game animals. The Piotr Gosciniak "Tracker" offers several options with its unique blade design and cleaver-style grind, the latter suitable for cutting cordage or even used with a baton for chopping purposes. Tomasz Dziubinski's "Nomad" is another example of a serious tactical fixed blade that will perform tough tasks. Both the Tracker and Nomad feature black Cerakote-finished blades.

Then there are the sexiest tactical knives—sub-hilt fighters, my favorite type, and my favorite maker of this style is Dave Broadwell. Dave's limited edition "Vanguard Guardian" is highlighted by its integral titanium guard and sub-hilt. The knife also features a blade fuller, or what some refer to as a blood groove. A fuller provides several advantages to a blade. It lightens it because of the groove in the steel, yet it also stiffens the blade by providing what is referred to as a second spine.

Decreasing the blade's contact area with the cutting medium, through the fuller or blood groove design element, reduces friction and provides a smoother cut. Proper placement of the fuller can also improve the knife's center of balance, optimizing handling.

Speaking of sexy, who doesn't love well-proportioned curves? Phillip Patton's "Vanguard Cheetah" features a sexy recurved blade with a more traditional guard and sub-hilt.

This article wouldn't be complete without custom tactical fixed blades incorporating military design influences. For that, I give you the "Spectra" daggers by Rafal Kolakowski. They are sleek, compact, and built for serious use. The "Paladin II" fighter from Michal Komorovsky exhibits sleek styling, a fuller and black DLC blade coating. The contoured, black canvas Micarta handle provides excellent ergonomics. Phillip Patton's "Vanguard Intrepid Fighter" adds design elements to the traditional fighting knife. Serrations behind the guard allow your thumb to control the blade better. The handle has vertical striations, giving the user an even better grip.

Final Thoughts

Do your research. Understand what you would like the knife to be able to do. Blade shape and length, steel choice, balance, and handle ergonomics are all important considerations. Because of all the options available in custom tactical fixed blades, you can truly get the right tool for the job. □

The Hawk Knives Shortcut has taken the industry-standard 2.4-inch utility blade and elevated it to "blue-collar splendor." No mystery here, the company has a reputation for extremely high-quality custom work and "thinking outside the box cutter."

Blue-Collar Splendor

The rise of replaceable blade technology and the utility knife.

By Pat Covert

The knife industry has seen many offshoots and niches since modern tactical knives burst onto the scene in the early 1990s, spreading their design and technological influences far and wide. One genre that has become particularly strong in recent years is the replaceable-blade knife, inherently designed to allow users to replace worn-out blades with new ones and even change blade styles. The concept is not new. Gerber has offered such blade-swapping ability on fixed blades and folders for years, but it has never caught on in the public realm.

When new concepts become popular in the knife industry, you can bet manufacturers jump on board, many times *en masse*. Look no further than the Michael Walker LinerLock that took modern tactical folders by storm in the early 1990s.

The utility knife category comprises two types of blades: proprietary replaceable blades manufactured for a specific knife and common replacement utility blades readily available on the market today. In recent years, Scalpel blades from the medical industry have gained traction with manufacturers of hunting and fishing knives, some with success and others testing the market.

Hawk Knives released the Shortcut utility knife in late 2022 and has been selling out of limited-edition runs ever since. The Shortcut is one of a continuous stream of knives produced by the father and son team that has garnered a reputation as being one of the most imaginative in the cutlery industry for over a decade. Grant Hawk, the founder of Hawk Knives, sadly passed away in November 2023, but fortunately left his son, Gavin, with years of collaborative imagination and engineering know-how under his belt. Indeed, the Shortcut was dreamed up and executed by Gavin.

"The Shortcut wasn't just another knife project for me," Gavin states. "It was about solving a real problem I saw in the knife community. I noticed people spending big bucks on knives, but then being scared to use them because blades wear out. So, I thought, 'Why not make a high-end utility knife where the blade—the only part that really wears down—is replaceable?' That's how the Shortcut came to be."

The Shortcut is essentially a custom folding utility knife built like a tank. It is designed to use the ubiquitous standard-sized 2.4-inch trapezoidal utility knife blade with two notches at top that is sold around the world.

The custom Teale Designs XL Utility Knife is 7 3/8 inches overall and 4 11/16 inches closed. Logan Thompson hand-machines, assembles and finishes each knife.

With its REDI model, Havalon Knives offers a nice alternative for hunters and other outdoors enthusiasts. The folder is available in both plain-edge and serrated blade options.

As for the Shortcut itself, "It's made from titanium, with my signature grip clip, and uses a Torx driver for blade changes to ensure a tight fit, unlike those loose quick-change systems that only allow access to half the blade's potential," Gavin said. "The latch lock I developed adds this cool 'flick to close the blade' feature, making it not just functional but fun."

Svelte Folder

Other pertinent specifications for the Shortcut include an overall length of 6.2 inches, a handle length of 4 inches, and a weight of 2.258 ounces, typical of a svelte folder in today's everyday-carry (EDC) market. Gavin meant for the replaceable-blade Shortcut to be carried, thus including a machined, spring-loaded 2.5-inch titanium tip-up pocket clip on the backside of the handle.

"Now, folks can carry a $475 knife, use it as hard as they want, and keep that premium feel without worrying about the blade. It's been a hit, and I'm already diving into more designs, including the Shortcut 2.0, which is still in the works without a final name, and a folding scalpel knife," he said.

To carry it daily or not for EDC? That is the question, and it's totally up to the user. The straight-edged utility blade, much like similar flat-edged Wharncliffe style edges, is considered one of the hardest-working blade shapes in the industry, so the functional aspect is proven. The Hawk Knives Shortcut is a high-end custom piece, especially for the category, but the Hawks have never walked the straight and narrow, and that's just how their customers like it.

Logan Thompson is a young up-and-coming knifemaker who grew up on social media, and if you don't partake in such forms of communication, chances are his name draws a blank. Logan's company, Teale Designs Tools, LLC, is a one-man outfit out of Virginia Beach, Virginia, and I ran across him on Etsy, an arts and handcrafts website that has a surprising number of knife and related tool listings.

You might say Logan was born with a knife in hand. "One of my brothers was a small engine mechanic while I was in high school," he said. "He always carried a multi-tool and knife for his work, and he sparked my interest in pocket tools. Since then, I have carried some sort of knife or multi-tool on me daily.

"Fast forward to college, and I became interested in computer-aided design [CAD]. I got my bachelor's degree in mechanical engineering from Virginia Commonwealth University, and my first professional job out of college was designing robotic systems and tooling. I did a lot of hands-on work on the production floor, of course carrying my knife and multi-tool. I had several other design positions ranging from small packaging systems to large 150-ton railroad recovery cranes. In 2015, I moved back to my hometown of Virginia Beach and took a job as a manufacturing engineer."

Logan wanted to be his own boss. He delved into woodworking for a while, but it wasn't exactly what he sought, so he pivoted to making pry bars for an interesting niche market populated by the younger set.

"Around 2018, I switched gears again, started Teale Designs Tools, LLC, and began manufacturing pocket tools from my CAD designs," he said.

The Hawk Knives Shortcut is basically a utility knife on steroids, and with a titanium frame for good measure. The utility blade of your choice pivots out of Gavin Hawk's signature "grip clip" with all the style and grace of a gent's folder.

Bit by the Knife Bug

Initially, Logan built tools, but the knife bug bit him harder, so he progressed to fixed blades and eventually folding knives. He has a distinct style, or should I say two, for his folders. One is a straightforward folder with plain steel and titanium parts, and the other features anodized titanium. A neat feature on his fixed blades is that users can set the retention of the sheaths to their preference by adjusting a single screw. Each fixed blade can be loosely sheathed or fully locked into its sheath for safety or travel reasons. The design also allows multiple carry options, from a tactical belt clip to a metal belt clip or even a deep-carry pocket sheath. Logan offers Kydex sheaths, which he says have gained in popularity.

"Around 2019, I started designing the replaceable-blade fixed utility knives. The main goal was to find the best geometry to secure the blade while still allowing an easy change-out when needed," he said. "Once I got that dialed in, I needed to determine the most efficient way for people to carry them. I wanted something a bit different than a leather sheath or large holster. I kind of stumbled upon the design and materials after several attempts.

"My first utility folders were made in 2021. The first knives were simple locking folders with push buttons to both release and close the blades. I was pleasantly surprised by the number of customers who were interested in this type of lock. However, I personally wanted something that had a different locking system on it. I was inspired by a maker whose business name is Snecx Design Lab, out of Malaysia, and who developed a unique locking system he called the 'Superlock.' It was unlike anything I had ever seen. Instead of a detent ball and a liner or frame lock, the mechanism he created controlled both closing and the locking of the knife. I reached out to Snecx to ask about utilizing his locking mechanism in my utility blade design and he gave me the green light."

Since 2022, Logan has been making folders using this locking mechanism.

Curious, I had to ask about autos. "Yes, I do have an automatic utility folder planned," he said. "There are some prototype parts sitting in the shop as I write this. I also have a slip-joint version in the works. I left my engineering job in December 2024 to run Teale Designs Tools full-time and am excited to see what comes out of the shop in the future."

Several years ago, a spate of major manufacturers jumped into the replaceable blade market for hunting and fishing knives, and I remembered asking myself at the time, *What's up with this?* So, I followed the market segment, wrote a few articles and reviews, and being the sponge that I am for all things that cut, I embraced it. It didn't take long, and I found out why.

Havalon Knives, a subsidiary of one of the world's largest medical scalpel suppliers, was already dabbling heavily in the fishing supply market and was making big inroads into the hunting knife end of the market. The company offers both replaceable standard medical and dedicated hunting and fishing blades of its own design. Other companies manufacturing replaceable-blade knives are Gerber Blades and Outdoor Edge. I suggest doing a Google search for what's available, as it can change yearly.

The replaceable-blade segment of the industry is a viable market with a big upside that just hasn't reached its full potential yet. But make no mistake about it, blue-collar splendor is here to stay! □

Logan Thompson's first knives under his business name, Teale Designs Tools, LLC, were fixed blades, and he established his look early on. Meanwhile, a cottage industry was springing up in the aftermarket for cool versions of utility blades.

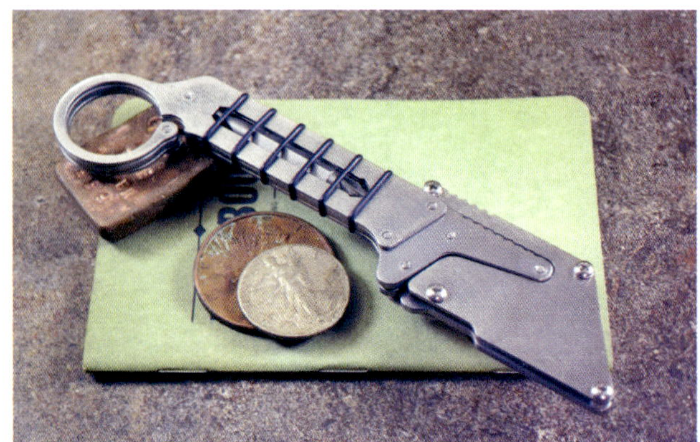

Today's Boomers Are Next Gen's *Knife Legends*

Four renowned knifemakers tell stories that would otherwise go untold.

By Jason Fry

There are times in life when nostalgia and wonder are especially poignant. As we age, we begin to lose grandparents and parents to the march of time. Even in this age of social media and technology, many of the stories never told are lost to time. The knifemaking world is no different.

I remember my first Knifemaker's Guild Show, in 2013, meeting Warren Osborne and seeing the memorial table of Ted Dowell, who had just passed away. I recall hearing names like Bob Loveless and Buster Warenski, men who passed before I even made my first knife. I remember names like Tony Bose and Joe Kious, knifemakers who were alive in my time, but whom I never met. Curious by nature, I sometimes ponder what it was like to sit with these men and shoot the breeze, talking about life, knifemaking and everything in between.

There's a saying, "The best time to plant a tree is 20 years ago, but the second-best time is today." I reached out to four experienced knifemakers with a goal of capturing their stories. When I did, one of the makers, Jerry Fisk, told me that "experienced" was "a real nice way to say old." As one generation passes the torch to another, we sometimes forget that, in earlier times, the experienced generation struggled in many of the same ways, dealt with some of the same problems, and overcame similar challenges as we do. Read on for the stories of four top-tier knifemakers, stories that would otherwise go untold.

The history of custom knives has no specific beginning or end. Much like a family tree, there's always an older ancestor, and often there is an expectation that the tree will continue to grow by adding new offspring. The hand-me-down transmission of knifemaking skills is similar, in that each current maker has mentors and hopefully some apprentices as well, building a thread that can later be traced both forward and backward.

One thread of this story begins in central Utah. At a Boy Scouts meeting in 1966, a young man named Steve Johnson was introduced to knifemaking by his Boy Scout Explorer advisor, Gil Hibben, who had recently opened a shop in Manti. Needing a job, it wasn't long before Steve began working in Gil's shop as a helper. "I didn't really have any knifemaking skills, so I spent at least the first two months at the bandsaw," Steve says.

Their relationship grew to include hunting, fishing and Kenpo Karate. They once rode motorcycles to Long Beach, California, to a Karate tournament sponsored by Ed Parker, one of the great martial arts practitioners and founder of Ed Parker's Kenpo Karate. That bike ride with Steve on a 160cc and Gil astride a 250 or 350cc Honda is another story! Gil was the boss, but he worked right alongside Steve and the other three or four shop workers, treating everyone well, and their friendships have endured to this day.

Also living nearby were two other knifemakers, Harvey Draper and Buster Warenski. Eventually,

Steve went to work for Draper on a part-time basis for several years as he attended college. Draper introduced Steve to Buster. Steve recalls, "I used to get depressed when I'd visit Buster because he was so skilled and talented. If he couldn't do something, he'd simply read up on it and learn how and then perform the task to perfection. I still can't even approach his work, but I have a bit more confidence now, I guess, thanks to all the help these makers gave me."

Partnership Formed

It was about that time that Rod "Caribou" Chappel visited the shop. During a successful fox hunt, a partnership was formed. Looking for a job opportunity, Steve moved for a year to Spokane, Washington, to work with Chappel. Within a year, they'd "had about enough of each other," and Steve started looking for another opportunity. In 1971, A.G. Russell heard that Loveless was looking for skilled help and connected Steve with Bob. Steve took advantage of the opportunity, arriving at Loveless' shop about the same time as the very first pallet of the now legendary 154CM stainless steel.

Steve Johnson's version of a "Big Bear" sub-hilt fighter is almost more recognizable than the work of his old partner and originator of the design, Bob Loveless. (SharpByCoop photo)

I asked Steve if there was some secret old-time recipe for the heat treat. He said that they had ground out the first 10 or 20 blades and taken them to the local heat-treat company with the instructions to "follow the manufacturer's recommendations." Like many a "good old boy," the heat treater thought he could do better. The result was that the first steel came out soft. When all else fails, follow the directions, and so the second time the heat treater used liquid nitrogen after the quench, and the cold treatment solved the hardness problem. It was also about this time that Steve joined The Knifemakers' Guild.

A head-on car crash resulting in significant injuries caused him to leave the Loveless shop in 1974. Steve finished his education degree during his recovery, but there were no teaching jobs available, so he opened his own knife shop in 1975. Steve says that knifemaking over nearly 60 years was the sole support for his wife, Dorothy, and their seven children. He credits the Guild and the Art Knife Invitational for introducing him to Italian collectors, who for many years made up a significant portion of his sales and orders.

Let's circle back now to the man at the beginning of Steve's story, Hibben. As the patriarch of this story, 90 years old by the time you're reading this, he's well known and well-traveled. His love for knives began when he first saw the 1952 film "The Iron Mistress." Gil's background includes a stint in the Navy and being a machinist at a Boeing factory. In those days, there were no guilds, no knife magazines, and not much of the equipment we take for granted today. Gil was the first person to apply a mirror finish to 440C "way back when." He was entirely self-taught because, in his time, there were not many people around to teach the art of knifemaking.

Gil credits his big break to *Guns & Ammo* magazine and the editors who put his knives on front covers in September 1965 and July 1968. He's perhaps most famous for making the iconic knives for the "Rambo III" and "Rambo" (fourth in the franchise) movies, as well as "The Expendables" franchise. When I asked Gil how that came about, he said it was all Sylvester Stallone. Sly had been buying Hibben's knives at gun shows, and they met for the first time at a show in California. They hit it off, and things escalated from there. Stallone had worked previously with Jimmy Lile but wanted the Rambo III knife to resemble a Hibben bowie that was in his collection, and so he photocopied both sides of the knife and faxed the pictures. Jimmy and Gil remained friends, and the rest is history.

There may be some backstabbing in the knife industry, but Gil holds the distinction of having stabbed himself in the back! During a knife-throwing demonstration while he was working at Silver Dollar City in Branson, Missouri, he threw a knife, then turned back to speak to the crowd. The knife didn't stick in the target but instead bounced back and stabbed Gil near his kidneys, and that was the end of knife throwing at Silver Dollar City. Later, in 1985, Gil worked on a big, heavy belt buckle fantasy knife. He heard that voice in his head say, "You're tired, don't pick that up again," but like many of us, he kept going anyway. It wasn't long before the grinder grabbed that heavy knife and threw it right through his thigh.

Industry Pioneer

Hibben is an industry pioneer and is credited with the first successful custom/factory knife collaboration. The deal was partially brokered by Houston Price, who connected Hibben with United Cutlery in 1987 to mass produce a version of the Rambo III knife. Hibben insisted that the reproduction be smaller than the originals and that it be marked "designed by Gil Hibben" instead of having a true Hibben tang stamp. Hibben has done design collaborations with United ever since. He is a 6th-degree black belt in Kenpo Karate, through which he also designed the "Parker," a special fighting knife for his black belt thesis project. As his instructor, Parker later had Gil make and deliver a knife to Elvis Presley.

Are these knives from the 1920s or today? Bill Ruple perfectly captures the classic style in a trio of slip-joint folders. (Eric Eggly, PointSeven Studios photo)

Gil was a longtime member of The Knifemakers' Guild, including being president of the organization from 2006-2013. He was also an Art Knife Invitational member and good friends with Phil Lobred. He even lived in Phil's basement for a while. Gil has been inducted into six different halls of fame, but says that's only because he's lived so long.

Meanwhile, back in the 1960s, at a farm in southwest Arkansas, 13-year-old Jerry Fisk sat at his family dinner table for a rite of passage. When they each turned 13, the four Fisk boys were given a bottle calf, and from that point forward, if they wanted anything beyond basic food and shelter, they had to earn it. On a 6th-grade field trip to Old Washington, Arkansas, Jerry saw his first demonstration by a knifemaker and blacksmith. He remembered that his grandfather had a forge and an anvil, but also that Grandpa had enough sense not to let young Jerry set things on fire.

After years of hard work doing odd jobs, mowing grass, farm work, and shoveling "glue," he was asked to take a part over to the local machine shop for repairs. He found the machinist sitting on a chair inside a shady building. Figuring that was better than shoveling in the sun, Jerry went to trade school in Hope, Arkansas, to become a machinist. He later did die work for the Case factory in Nashville, Arkansas. At work, he'd be given a worn-out die and a complete knife made from a similar die and then be instructed to replicate the pattern for a new die.

Jerry made his first knife in 1972, in difficult circumstances. His son had some medical problems, and the bill was $32,000, while Jerry's annual salary was only $16,000. Jerry said that he'd never heard of a knifemaker other than Buck or Case, and he knew they sold their knives for $10-$15 each, so he thought he'd better price himself below the professionals. He figured out that a $10 bar of steel could make two $8 knives and nearly double his money. The first few he made had handles held on with Phillips head screws!

"I didn't know any better," he says.

The first professional knifemaker he met was Bill Bagwell. They were members at the same hunt club, and Bill offered to teach Jerry knifemaking if Jerry would, in turn, teach him to squirrel hunt. That's some backwoods barter at its finest. Over the years, Jerry and "Bags" had a great friendship, filled with knives, hunting, fishing and a good measure of practical jokes.

Jerry describes a hunting trip where he met a fellow with a "knife with wrinkles all over it." Turns out, it was a Sid Burt damascus knife. Jerry didn't see much use for a knife with wrinkles. He said "art" was a guy who lived down the street, and a knife was a tool. *What's the point in having a bowie knife?* he wondered at the time. Eventually, Jerry would come around to both damascus steel and bowies, although he claims it took him two weeks to learn how to start a coal fire, and a week of hammering to forge his first knife. I get the distinct impression that perhaps Jerry likes to embellish his stories a bit. He told me one time that he had a knife so sharp it would cut my phone bill in half!

The Cheerleader

Jerry's approach to mentoring was shaped by his upbringing. A few lessons, and you'd better figure it out for yourself. He was instrumental in teaching bladesmithing in Brazil, which is now a hotbed of excellent knifemakers. By the third year, he traveled to South America to teach, and he said he "pretty much quit teaching and became a cheerleader." As for his own personal cheerleaders, he credits B.R. Hughes, a fan of Jerry's work, for teaching him about pricing, sales and marketing. While Fisk did not get a college degree, he went to night school and took courses in journalism, accounting and business management. Jerry says he'd ask anyone a question if they'd take time to listen, and that's how he met Warenski, and there's the thread that connects Utah and Arkansas knifemakers.

Buster and Bill Moran were instrumental in Jerry being named a "National Living Treasure" in 1999. The process included state governor nominations and a national contest. Jerry says he figures Bill and Buster should have won before he did, but that's not the way it panned out. Jerry was active in The Knifemakers' Guild, the American Bladesmith Society and the Custom Knife Collectors' Association (CKCA).

It was through the CKCA that he first began using historical artifacts in his work. He won an award that provided funds to innovate and explore new techniques. States and countries have their own histories, and every history has items and materials associated with it. Jerry has used material as diverse as steel from the World Trade Center and wood from David Crockett's childhood home to fashion fine knives. He shared this idea with several other knifemakers, me included, and remains a great cheerleader.

Bill Ruple goes all in with his five-blade sowbelly, featuring Mike Tyre feather damascus and detailed file work. (Caleb Royer photo)

Gut hook fixed blades go in and out of fashion, but this Bob Loveless/Steve Johnson example is timeless. (SharpByCoop photo)

From Pleasanton, Texas, Bill Ruple's work sells on the market for more than peanuts these days, but peanuts are where it all began. Bill and his brother partnered in a peanut farming operation, which inherently has boom-and-bust cycles and yearly off-seasons. In the slow times of the year, Bill started making knives under the watchful eye of Pat West. Texas is full of cowboys, roping arenas, and two-bladed trappers, and Pat was the local knifemaker. Building his first knife in 1988, like many makers, Bill started with utilitarian patterns and worked his way up as time went on. By the mid-1990s, he'd become a regular at knife shows and made a name for himself in the slip-joint pocketknife industry. The farming work cycle kept him busy in the summer and fall, and slow in the winter and spring, so he made knives during the slow times.

Tony Bose was a custom knife collaborator who worked with Case Cutlery from 1998 until his death in 2020. Bill met Tony at the Guild Show in Orlando sometime around 1992. One early piece of Tony's advice that stands out involved a knife that Bill brought to him for critique. Tony's reply was that "Symmetry isn't where you buried your grandpa."

Bill says, "We got to know each other over the years, and it got to where we'd talk on the phone almost every morning. He was a big influence on me. Every time I would see his stuff, I'd be blown away by it, and I would think, man, I want to be *this* guy. I want to be that good."

Now that he has a design contract with Case since Bose's death, Bill *is* that guy. With Reese Bose's permission, Bill formed a relationship with Case, and, given the company's history of loyalty to its employees and partners, the odds are that it will last.

Much like Manti in the 1960s and 70s, South Texas has become a hotspot for knifemaking connections and instruction. One thing Bill learned from Pat West was a sense of responsibility to pass on knowledge. He is the patriarch of the "South Texas Slip-Joint Cartel," which has now expanded to include makers from Oklahoma and even Australia.

The threads that connect these men, from Utah to Arkansas, Case Cutlery to South Texas, and through legends and stories of those who have passed, come together to form one, single, strong cord. To this cord are added the threads and connections from such legendary men to many of us who are active in the industry. As we, too, build connections between each other and those we teach, the cord grows ever stronger, ultimately binding us together into one common history of utility and craftsmanship in the form of knifemaking, an art as old as humanity. □

Gil Hibben is perhaps most famous for making the iconic knives for the "Rambo III" and "Rambo" (fourth in the franchise) movies, as well as "The Expendables" franchise. Sylvester Stallone had been buying knives like these Hibben bowie/fighters at gun shows, and the two men met for the first time at a show in California. They hit it off, and things escalated from there. Stallone had worked previously with Jimmy Lile but wanted the Rambo III knife to resemble a Hibben bowie that was in his collection, so he photocopied both sides of the knife and faxed the pictures. Jimmy and Gil remained friends, and the rest is history.

Created specifically for the 2022 Art Knife Invitational, Jerry Fisk's small bowie boasts a multi-layer damascus blade overlaid with 24-karat gold, deep-relief engraving with more inlaid gold, and a mammoth ivory handle. (SharpByCoop photo)

The Changing Face OF KNIFE SHOWS

One thing remains the same—personal connections with collectors are priceless.

By Rick Dunkerley

Sitting at 34,000 feet over the North Atlantic on my flight home from the 2024 C.I.C. (*Corporazione Italiana Coltellinai*) Show in Milan, Italy, I couldn't help but think of all the knife shows I've attended and how much things have changed over the years. I started making knives in the early 1980s, when my sales were all by word of mouth. My only exposure to other handmade knives was occasional visits to the shops of makers I heard about in magazine ads or read about in earlier editions of these *KNIVES* annual books.

Rick Dunkerley's Model 1 button-release folding dagger with a mosaic damascus blade won "Best Folder" and "Best in Show" at the 2021 International Custom Cutlery Exposition. Of sole authorship, the knife also showcases color-case-hardened mild steel bolsters with 24k-gold and fine silver inlays, and carved antique shell handle scales backed in gold leaf.

I attended a few of the early gun, knife and outdoor gear shows, and saw a few makers who were fashioning knives similar to my own hunting knives. In the early '90s, I attended my first knife event, the Oregon Knife Collectors Association Show, in Eugene, Oregon. To say that it was eye-opening is a huge understatement. Seeing the work of makers like Gay Rocha, Bill McHenry, J.D. Smith and Wayne Goddard, to name just a few, was a revelation as to what great handmade knives could be. This exposure to the highest level of handmade knives is, in my opinion, one of the biggest benefits of attending shows.

By seeing the work of top makers, a fair comparison between them and the quality of one's own work can be made. The resulting motivation is a great push for the aspiring maker and some of us old guys. Even after more than 30 years of doing shows, I am still motivated by the work of the great makers out there. In the mid-'90s, I attended my first East Coast Custom Knife Show. Walking into that room, I was shocked to see Buster Warenski, Gray Taylor, Jim Schmidt, Don Fogg and the rest of the greatest makers of that era. I honestly felt I didn't belong in the room with them. That feeling motivated me to push my work to new levels.

In 2015, I was invited to my first Art Knife Invitational, and those same feelings of not belonging were almost overwhelming in the presence of such incredible makers. These experiences have been instrumental in my developing new skills, and I believe most makers can benefit from exposure to peers whose skill levels are more highly developed. Shows provide that opportunity, along with the chance to talk to top-tier makers and have your work critiqued by the best in the business.

Social media and Internet sales have certainly affected shows over the last 20 years. The ability to purchase knives from the comfort of their desk chairs has enabled collectors to attend fewer shows and still pursue their knife passion. While this has opened a new market, I feel it has also lessened the personal nature of collecting. From a maker's standpoint, the personal interaction at a show can provide insight into a potential collector's likes and dislikes. Understanding the mindset of buyers can be invaluable. For the collector, the exchange is also a chance to understand the maker and the direction future work may take.

Rick Dunkerley (right) poses with his buddy Bill Ruple at BLADE Show Texas in 2023. Throughout his career, Dunkerley says he has felt somewhat intimidated walking into a knife show where legends like Ruple display wares such as this CPM 154 lockback whittler in stainless bolsters and stag handle scales. (SharpByCoop knife image)

Conversations I've had with knife enthusiasts and collectors have led to some of my favorite projects, and speaking to them in person adds to the entire experience. Shows also give the collector a chance to view multiple examples of a maker's work. A knife in hand may feel entirely different than what one would imagine from looking at a photograph. These interactions also help makers understand what collectors prefer in the knives they purchase. The body language of someone looking at and handling one of your knives can tell you as much as words. That's information that is not available during an online transaction.

As a knifemaker, it's easy to focus solely on overall sales at shows and forget about one-on-one exposure and interactions throughout the course of the event with potential buyers, as well as the long-term benefits of such interpersonal communication. Optimistically, a maker knows how much money they will make if they completely sell out of knives. Realistically, most won't always deplete their inventory, but being there in front of collectors is a big part of the business.

Discovering New Material

Years ago, I was told that the best makers use the most high-end materials. I took that to heart, and over the years, I've used shows to purchase most of the materials I now use. The ability to see and inspect material is critical in discovering the building blocks for the types of knives that I make. Most shows, and especially large ones like the BLADE

From left to right, swordmaker Peter Johnsson, engraver Barry Lee Hands and legendary knifemaker Harvey Dean are deep in conversation at the 2022 Art Knife Invitational. Johnsson's "Harbinger" sword showcases an 820-layer damascus blade with undulating grooves, a carved and patinated iron guard and pommel, and a leather grip with cast and carved sterling silver ferrules. Dean's dog bone dagger features a gold-inlaid feather damascus blade, pearl handle, domed gold pins and engraving. (SharpByCoop knife and sword photos)

Posing with Enrica (left) and Dario Quartini at the 2024 C.I.C. Show in Milan, Italy, it was during the airplane ride on his way back home to the United States that Rick Dunkerley (center) says he couldn't help but think of all the knife shows he's attended and how much things have changed over the years.

Show, BLADE Show Texas, and BLADE Show West, are like supermarkets of knifemaking materials. With natural handle material, I prefer to buy only after I have inspected it in person. I've also discovered new material at shows that I probably would never have tried if I'd only seen it in a photo.

Handle material, blade steel, sheath material and hardware are all available at shows, providing one-stop shopping for knifemakers. Turning the pages of this book, you will see hundreds of photos of knives by makers from around the world. Many of those photos were taken at knife shows. Most of the larger shows have at least one photographer in attendance. The largest events will almost certainly have several

A young Rick Dunkerley attends an early 1990s Oregon Knife Collectors Association Show in Eugene. "To say that it was eye-opening is a huge understatement," Dunkerley says. "Seeing the work of makers like Gay Rocha, Bill McHenry, J.D. Smith and Wayne Goddard, to name just a few, was a revelation as to what great handmade knives could be."

professional photographers set up for business all weekend, providing a great opportunity for makers to develop relationships with them. It's a chance for them to discuss how they'd like a photo to represent their work and what details the maker wants to capture. Collectors can also have their knives photographed at shows and not deal with the hassle and stress of shipping valuable blades.

Documenting collections is great for business in general and can also help the collector for insurance purposes. The atmosphere at shows has and will continue to change as the market for handmade knives evolves around trends in their popularity. With online buying becoming an ever-increasing segment of the knife market, it seems some collectors don't attend as many shows or may have quit attending them altogether.

When collector numbers drop at shows, the number of big-name makers tends to drop as well. What was somewhat of a show circuit 20 years ago has become a more hit-and-miss proposition recently, though you wouldn't know it by attending the BLADE Show in Atlanta. That's more like a smorgasbord of the hottest knives and makers in the world. It's all about connections between collectors and makers, photographers and exhibitors, Knife of the Year contestants and judges, demonstrations and audience members, classes and students, and masters and apprentices.

Larger shows still attract good numbers of collectors, and renowned makers will always be a draw for them. For smaller shows, I believe that makers need to be more proactive in promoting attendance. Some makers seem hesitant about inviting their collectors to knife exhibitions. Most collectors are not buying exclusively from one maker, and I feel getting my collectors to attend shows helps everyone. This crossover of buyers is good for the blade business.

Since that first Oregon Knife Collectors Association Show over 30 years ago, I've exhibited my handmade wares at over 100 shows in the United States and abroad. My reasons for attending shows have evolved over that time, and although it's nice to sell out, I'm more concerned with maintaining and building relationships with potential collectors and giving them a chance to view my work and talk about their knife interests. Those conversations have been a highlight for me and invaluable in understanding the collectors who love what we do.

I've developed longstanding friendships because of those conversations, not just impersonal business relationships. So, for the makers, get out there and try exhibiting at a few of the countless knife shows that are held annually. You never know when the biggest collector in the world could walk by, so remember, you only get one chance to make a first impression. And for the collectors, come out and meet the makers you've been reading about and whose work you've been admiring in print and online photos. I guarantee we will all have some fun. □

Rick Dunkerley says this was a very intimidating group of knifemakers to meet at his first Art Knife Invitational in 2015. (Francesco Pachi photo)

If there's any doubt about the future of the custom knife industry, look no further than the younger generation, and you realize it's in good hands. Observe not only the modern makers themselves, but also the knives they're fashioning, the materials they're using and the forms and functions they're creating. I love it that the same group of modern knifemakers and bladesmiths utilize ancient ivory and bog oak, and composite stones, resin spacers and super synthetics. They embrace the new and old, borrowing elements from each and making them their own.

The folding knives in the "Fresh Takes on Folders" chapter are so new and functionally sound that they need little introduction, just their own viewing in this art gallery of handmade blades. The "Sizzlin' Chef's Knives" parade modern forms and high-tech materials, and the "Take-Down Knives" are engineered by some of the most mechanically inclined minds in the knifemaking arena. Not only are they building complicated contraptions, but also tearing them down, rebuilding them, and making it as simple as possible for their customers to do the same.

The daggers are done right, the reproductions classically styled, the bowies best in class, the hunters on-point and the fighters ripped. The swords slay, and the pocketknives display pinpoint precision. These knives are currently trending, and they're as hot as a steel billet still smoldering after being pulled from the coal forge.

Cowboy Knives

It's nice to see handmade entries in the subgenre of cowboy knives, blades that are first and foremost utilitarian in look and performance, easy to carry and with a wrangler or Western influence. These are knives that the makers designed to be worn in belt sheaths or jeans pockets for easy one-handed access to the edged tools when necessary.

The blades are built to be employed daily, and most dawns and dusks, for myriad chores and impromptu tasks, mainly outdoors, or in sheds, barns, stables or stanchions. Few owners of cowboy knives leave their homesteads without them, and the blades' use, maintenance and sharpening are second nature to the owners.

Cowboy up with what looks to be a hot new category, or one reborn out of necessity or popularity. Whatever the reason that modern custom makers are building cowboy knives for their clients, it's always a good time to ride the open plains and prairies, following the doggies and whistling a tune while you wrangle a stray cow or calf.

« DAVID FLEMING: The everyday carry cowboy knife enlists a hollow-ground CPM 154 blade and a Rocky Mountain sheep horn handle. *(Jocelyn Frasier Photography)*

« KEVIN CROSS: When you sport a hobo nickel buttcap, you're one sharp number, dressed here in Delbert Ealy damascus, a nickel silver guard and oosic handle. *(SharpByCoop photo)*

« CHRIS GARDNER: The "carry bowie" ingratiates itself via a 5160 blade, stainless guard and mammoth ivory handle scales. *(Jocelyn Frasier Photography)*

» DAVID TABER: The "Diamond Edge Cattle Knife" comes in hollow-ground CPM 154 blades and bark elephant ivory handle scales. *(SharpByCoop photo)*

» CHRIS TAYLOR: The "Boston Mountain Blade" is equipped for rough terrain in 1095 steel with a visible hamon (temper line), a sambar stag handle, brass guard and vintage Micarta spacers. *(Mitchell D. Cohen Photography)*

DAVID FLEMING: Rocky Mountain bighorn sheep handle scales hold the cowboy knife/EDC securely, here in a 3-inch upswept, hollow-ground and recurved CPM 154 stainless blade. *(Jocelyn Frasier Photography)*

Rich Ancient Ivory

» **JIM DUNLAP:** A three-blade sowbelly arrives in rich ancient ivory. *(Mitchell D. Cohen Photography)*

« **BILL THORNE:** Mammoth ivory and twist damascus make up the beautiful bulk of the 10.25-inch bowie. *(Jocelyn Frasier Photography)*

« **BRUCE BARNETT:** The centerpiece of a four-blade CPM 154 stainless Congress pocketknife is the fossil mammoth ivory handle bookended by Nic Gregson-engraved stainless bolsters. *(Rod Hoare photo)*

« **GRAYSON JENNINGS:** Mammoth ivory handle scales lend warmth to a Wharncliffe trapper in etched A2 blades. *(Mitchell D. Cohen Photography)*

SCOTT GALLAGHER: Some lucky folding knife lover will own this mosaic damascus wonder in mammoth ivory handle scales. *(Jocelyn Frasier Photography)*

BILLY BOB SOWELL: A tasteful damascus and ancient ivory folder cuts to the quick. *(Mitchell D. Cohen Photography)*

BILL OGDEN: The mini Kwaiken model showcases an Alabama Damascus blade and a rare caramel-color mammoth ivory handle. *(SharpByCoop photo)*

SCHUYLER LOVESTRAND: The F-2 sub-hilt fighter makes good use of CPM 154 steel, stainless and mammoth ivory. *(SharpByCoop photo)*

» GARY LANGLEY: A CPM 154 sub-hilt fighter is all the better for those mammoth ivory handle scales. *(Jocelyn Frasier Photography)*

« BOBBY HOUSE: Richness built into the small trapper includes a CPM 154 blade, "Wasp Nest" damascus bolsters, a hound's tooth shield and ancient blonde mammoth ivory handle scales. *(Mitchell D. Cohen Photography)*

» MASON BRANDA: The mammoth tusk handle crackles on a 7-inch chef's knife with 80CrV2-and-15N20-damascus blade and Richlite frame. *(Jocelyn Frasier Photography)*

JOHN CHAPMAN: The AEB-L drop-point hunter with cross-cut mammoth tusk handle will steal the heart after piercing it. *(SharpByCoop photo)*

» ROBERT YOUNG: A Bob Loveless-style "Big Bear" is unblemished in CPM 154 and stainless steels and cross-cut mammoth ivory scales. *(Jocelyn Frasier Photography)*

« DOMINICK GOLD: The mammoth tusk and buffalo horn handle of a chef's knife is a head turner, accompanied by an Alabama Damascus blade. *(Mitchell D. Cohen Photography)*

CHRIS RICHARDSON: Leapin' lizards, the lockback folder comes alive in mammoth ivory handle scales and an "angel skin" coral thumb stud. *(Jocelyn Frasier Photography)*

» BRIAN EFROS: The "Sonic Doom" commands the room in a Mike Norris damascus blade, zirconium bolsters and mammoth ivory handle scales. *(Mitchell D. Cohen Photography)*

» NOAH SMITH: Mammoth ivory makes a statement on a CPM 154 sowbelly trapper. *(Mitchell D. Cohen Photography)*

« BOB MERZ: Wes Griffin gold inlay and engraving bookends the mammoth ivory handle scales of a CPM 154 lockback folder. *(Jocelyn Frasier Photography)*

« DAVID LISCH: The layered mosaic damascus blade is complemented by fossilized walrus handle scales and a "shop rats" forged "tail and sphincter" pommel. *(SharpByCoop photo)*

« CHAD J. JONES: A tiny knife (3 inches overall) has much going on, such as a "Gorgan Flower" damascus blade, ivory G-10 bolsters and blue mammoth tusk handle scales. *(Jocelyn Frasier Photography)*

» COREY HOLLEY: A clean, straight-arrow dagger features N690 stainless steel and fossil walrus ivory. *(Mitchell D. Cohen Photography)*

RHIDIAN GATRILL: As if CPM 154 split-back whittler pocketknives weren't impressive enough, add mammoth ivory handle scales to the mix. *(Jocelyn Frasier Photography)*

« JOHN H. DAVIS: The tactical folder is dressed respectfully in Alliema Damax stainless damascus, mokume-gane, anodized titanium and rich mammoth tusk ivory. *(SharpByCoop photo)*

JUSTIN CHENAULT: The coffin-handle vest bowie is done up in a mokume-gane guard and mammoth ivory grip. *(Mitchell D. Cohen Photography)*

DON HANSON III: Mammoth ivory makes a statement on a trapper that also features a damascus blade forged by the maker.

(Mitchell D. Cohen Photography)

SHAYNE CARTER: A bow-to-thee-worthy bowie is immersed in "Turkish Ws" twist damascus and mammoth ivory.

(Jocelyn Frasier Photography)

STEVE HILL: "The Wizard of Awes" showcases rainbow colors in the bolsters, a random-pattern damascus blade heat colored to resemble a yellow brick road leading to the "Emerald City" set in the thumb stud, and ancient mammoth ivory handle scales.

« MATT DAVIS:
Blue mammoth ivory makes a bold statement on a 4.5-inch EDC knife with a stainless blade featuring the maker's trademarked The Davis Grind. *(Jocelyn Frasier Photography)*

» J.W. RANDALL:
Well-executed material makeup on an EDC/hunter includes a dizzying damascus blade, Joe Mason guard engraving and mammoth ivory handle scales. *(Jocelyn Frasier Photography)*

» D.R. DAVIS:
Excuse me while I whip out this three-blade sowbelly pocketknife in CPM 154 steel and mammoth ivory. *(Mitchell D. Cohen Photography)*

Composite Stone & Resin Spacers

Well, what a winsome look that is—wood and G-10 knife handles with composite stone and resin spacers. Knifemakers carry on a culture of creativity by combining modern materials in ways not heretofore assembled, with stone and resin spacers acting as the colorful centerpieces of the collective creations.

They're the bowties of the knives, the shoulder sashes of the handles, the honor stripes of the grips and the marketing hooks for new custom blades. Buyers and collectors are the beneficiaries of a synthetic handle movement that shows no signs of slowing down. With ivory, pearl and even sambar stag becoming more difficult to come by, suppliers commission and make many materials that will appeal to the aesthetic sensibilities of knife artisans. It's amazing what can happen when an industry unites for a common cause—composite stone and resin spacers, that is.

« CHRIS JONES: The Japanese Wa-style octagonal curly maple handle of the stainless damascus Gyuto features spacers of Trustone and stainless steel, the latter engraved by Phil Dunn. *(Jocelyn Frasier Photography)*

» JORDAN DANZ: Choose the Woodcreek Hunter in a flat-ground Alabama damascus blade, colorful G-10 liners, and a Koa wood, green resin and white Corian handle. *(SharpByCoop photo)*

« JARRA BILLINGS: The Honesuki Japanese poultry knife cuts through the competition in a flat-ground Nitro-V blade, and a G-10 and Trustone handle. *(Rod Hoare photo)*

» ROBERT WAYMAN: The handle of a "Go-Mai" chopper with nickel and damascus cladding is a not-so-simple matter of cross-cut carbon fiber, G-10, malachite, fossilized brain coral and amboyna burl. *(SharpByCoop photo)*

» TYLER HACKBARTH: Turquoise Trustone and black G-10 spacers highlight the curly Koa handle of a Gyuto, this with a Mike Norris "Hornet's Nest" damascus blade. *(Jocelyn Frasier Photography)*

» JOSE SANTIAGO-CUMMINGS: To compete with the "Spirograph"-pattern stainless damascus blade, the maker assembled a cast of textured brass, buffalo horn, composite malachite, maple burl, fine silver and abalone shell characters. *(Jocelyn Frasier Photography)*

Sizzlin' Chef's Knives

« DAN TOMPKINS: The only thing that can rein in that gorgeous mosaic damascus blade of a Kiritsuke kitchen knife is an African blackwood handle with a damascus spacer. *(SharpByCoop photo)*

» MAK KELSAY: The Gyuto chef's knife bespeaks of tradition with the rough-forged 52100 blade and silver wire-inlaid hickory handle. *(Jocelyn Frasier Photography)*

» JASON ELLARD: The Tasmanian knifemaker hand forged a 1084 blade for an integral chef's knife with a black Micarta handle. *(BladeGallery.com photo)*

« BEN EUSTACE: The 15N20 blade with mustard patina is pleasing to the palate, as are the brass bolster and red morrell burl handle. *(Rod Hoare photo)*

» BRETT BENNETT: The copper handles of the damascus Gyuto and Santoku knives are die-formed and patinated. *(SharpByCoop photo)*

« KELLY FRASIER: No pared-down paring knife, it exhibits purple tamarind scales, purple G-10 liners and a 26C3 carbon steel blade in a mustard patina. *(Jocelyn Frasier Photography)*

» JOSHUA FISHER: An 8-inch chef's knife looks every bit the part in a Nitro-V stainless blade with a Shinogi grind and a vintage Westinghouse Micarta handle. *(BladeGallery.com photo)*

« MERT TANSU: With a convex-ground Wootz blade, walrus ivory bolster and maple burl handle, the Gyuto chef's knife is a looker. *(Rod Hoare photo)*

» JOSHUA FORAN: The wide damascus blade of a chef's knife terminates in an integral guard and a beautiful black ash burl handle. *(SharpByCoop photo)*

» MATT PARKINSON: Fusing a mosaic damascus blade with carved, gold-plated lower inlays, a bronze bolster and stabilized maple handle, perhaps the chef's knife is for fusion food pairings. *(SharpByCoop photo)*

» MARK SINCLAIR: A kitchen utility/petty knife is fashioned in a chevron-pattern damascus blade, stainless bolster and fossil walrus ivory handle. *(Rod Hoare photo)*

» IAN ROGERS: A long, thin damascus Gyuto is prepared for you today in a FatCarbon "Gold Dark Matter" bolster and a stabilized Hawaiian curly Koa handle. *(BladeGallery.com photo)*

» HAREY DEAN: The nicest slicer in the drawer features a "West Texas Wind" damascus blade, exhibition stag handle and engraved bolsters. *(Mitchell D. Cohen Photography)*

» DAVID HOEHLER: When you whip out the Western Gyuto in a blue acrylic resin and copper mesh handle, and 14C28N stainless blade, the sous chefs take notice. *(BladeGallery.com photo)*

» ANDREW SMITH: A "River of Fire" damascus blade will get the cooking juices flowing, accompanied by an amboyna burl handle. *(SharpByCoop photo)*

« SASHA ROSENFELD: A 26C3 "Spicy White" carbon steel blade was an appropriate choice for the Honyaki chef's knife handled in spalted Koa. *(BladeGallery.com photo)*

» FRANCOIS MAZIERES: The "Bunka" design damascus kitchen knife reveals an octagonal West Australian tiger eye guard, bronze spacer and black Mulga wood handle. *(Rod Hoare photo)*

« DEVIN RODRICK: A damascus bread knife is a tough pattern to tackle, executed beautifully here in an integral bolster and Arizona desert ironwood handle. *(BladeGallery.com photo)*

« WARREN THACKER: Dazzling damascus chef's knives are handled in similarly astounding stabilized California buckeye and curly birch handles. *(SharpByCoop photo)*

JOEY DELLO RUSSO:
A Santoku is fashioned with a 9-inch 80CrV2 and pure nickel blade, a nickel silver bolster, and a Richlite handle. *(Jocelyn Frasier Photography)*

ANDREW BONAVIA:
Forge marks are strategically left on the flat-ground W2 blade of a K-Tip kitchen knife, featuring an ebony handle with G-10 and ringed Gidgee spacers. *(Rod Hoare photo)*

CRISTIAN SILVA:
A black G-10 handle complete with red liners anchors the 9.7-inch hand-forged W2 blade of a Honyaki chef's knife. *(BladeGallery.com photo)*

KEVIN CROSS:
The long, slender Yanagiba Japanese chef's knife integrates an RWL-34 blade, G-10 guard and a Raffir-stabilized wood handle. *(SharpByCoop photo)*

TIM ROWLAND:
Two Gyuto chefs' knives sport differentially heat-treated blades with smoky temper lines, and stag and rosewood handles. *(SharpByCoop photo)*

» JOSH HULTS: Black ash wood and "Radial Ws" damascus spice up a 7-inch chef's knife. *(Jocelyn Frasier Photography)*

GREG MANDER: A Gyuto chef's knife with keyhole bolster incorporates a 200-layer damascus blade, and a figured redgum handle featuring damascus and brass inlays. *(Rod Hoare photo)*

« CASEY VILENSKY: A couple of kitchen-worthy chef's/choppers come in high-carbon steel blades and ebony and blackwood handles, one with a mammoth ivory spacer. *(SharpByCoop photo)*

» DAVE SKINNER: Mouthwatering elements include a hand-forged damascus san mai blade with VG-10 core, a nickel silver bolster, black G-10 spacer and a dyed and stabilized octagonal masur birch handle. *(BladeGallery.com photo)*

« COREY DUNLAP: Ingredients of a 9-inch chef's knife include a Corey Dunlap and Tony Immordino damascus blade, and a highly figured wood handle. *(SharpByCoop photo)*

« MARTIN MOENNING: The "King Eider Chef Knife" is a pretty bird with an A2 tool steel beak and vintage paper Micarta plumage. *(Jocelyn Frasier Photography)*

BILL BURKE: The Western-style Japanese petty kitchen knife exhibits a damascus blade, black Mulga wood handle and African blackwood bolster. *(BladeGallery.com photo)*

» MARDI MESHEJIAN: The maker dishes one out in a damascus blade, copper bolster and stabilized oak handle. *(SharpByCoop photo)*

» JORDAN BERTHELOT: Excuse me while I whip out my raindrop-pattern "TigerMai" chef's knife with stabilized box elder burl handle. *(BladeGallery.com photo)*

« KYLE DAILY: An 8-inch chef's knife features curly Koa handle scales set on white G-10 and black canvas Micarta liners via Micarta pins. *(Mitchell D. Cohen Photography)*

IBIS CUTLERY: This little sampler platter of chef's knives includes one in amboyna burl, blackwood and damascus (right), and a second in ebony, buffalo horn and W2 tool steel (left). *(SharpByCoop photo)*

» MATTHEW DONALDSON: A 15-inch swayback Gyuto is fashioned from a clad damascus blade with an 80CrV2 core, a tiger myrtle handle and black G-10 spacer. *(Rod Hoare photo)*

» JORDAN BUCKLEY: The food will just fall away from the "Explosion" pattern mosaic damascus blade of an 8-inch chef's knife in an antiqued bronze bolster and stabilized maple burl handle. *(BladeGallery.com photo)*

Born of the Bogs

Precious wood pulled from bogs after thousands of years of being submerged in murky depths, bog oak is prized for knife handles, and why wouldn't it be? The acid-rich, oxygen-poor environs of bogs change humble woods such as oak into something dark and mysterious, infused with history and lined with age.

The deep black and brown knife handles harness ancient secrets from the bog. Their stability and salinity are instilled through ages of formation, and their hardness harnessed from harsh surroundings that were once their home.

Breathe in the stale air and admire the aged complexions—bog oak bestows richness upon knife handles, infusing them with body and soul. The distant past permeates the palms of those who grip the bog oak hilts, transporting them to a time and place when edged tools were treasured and never taken for granted.

Born of the bogs, the knives bespeak honor and tradition.

» **MARK LAMBERT:** Gray and black bog oak anchors a ladder-pattern damascus hunter with a stainless guard. *(Jocelyn Frasier Photography)*

« **CHARLIE ELLIS:** The "North Star Petty" knife sports a combination "Gold Star" mosaic and "Jelly Roll" damascus blade, a sterling silver and Richlite guard and a bog oak handle. *(SharpByCoop photo)*

» ANDREW SMITH: The tricked-out tomahawk showcases a 1084-and-15N20-damascus head, bog oak haft and a mother-of-pearl inlay. *(Mitchell D. Cohen Photography)*

« DAVE SKINNER: A drop-dead-gorgeous damascus hunter is handled in a stippled bog oak grip. *(BladeGallery.com photo)*

LEE PARSONS: Stamped "Republic of Texas March 2nd 1836," the bowie blends a bog oak handle with a gold star inlay, brass fittings and a 1095 blade. *(Jocelyn Frasier Photography)*

STEPHAN FOWLER: The wickedly recurved blade is by Don Hanson, and the oak handle from an ancient bog. *(SharpByCoop photo)*

JEREMY MARSH: The "Celtic Assassin" slips out in a damascus blade, zirconium bolsters engraved by Johnathon Quill and 10,000-year-old Irish bog oak handle scales. *(Mitchell D. Cohen Photography)*

ROB LOGAN: An ancient bog oak spacer acts as a respite between the twist-damascus blade of a chef's knife and its amboyna burl handle. *(Jocelyn Frasier Photography)*

Fresh Takes on Folders

There are so many takes on folders, and each more modern, exotic, tactical, fresh, colorful, stealthy or fancy than the one that came before it. Tactical folders have evolved into high-tech folding knives made from materials that weren't available or known to knifemakers only 2, 5, 10 or 15 years ago.

Knifemaking materials and parts companies have sprung up overnight, catering to manufacturers and custom knifemakers who crave something new and beautiful. Functionality meets fanciful delight, and once again, knife enthusiasts and collectors are the beneficiaries of creative composition.

Add in a bolt lock, Hawk Lock, frame lock, BladeLock, toggle detent, locking liner or back lock, and now you've got a folder that works like a fixed blade and handles like a sports car. Titanium meets CarboQuartz where the FatCarbon bolsters join the Damasteel blades. These are no primitive pocketknives, but fresh takes on folders that have started a feverish knife-buying frenzy in an industry born ready for expansion.

GAVIN HAWK: Claws are appropriately carved into the carbon-fiber handle scales of the "Talon" folder with Hawk Lock and toggle detent. *(Mitchell D. Cohen Photography)*

MANUELE MESSORI: From the pearl-inlaid Damasteel blade to the contoured-handle frame, the folder is a fresh and flashy example. *(SharpByCoop photo)*

BOBBY HOUSE: Here's a swell-end jackknife in a ladder-pattern damascus blade, stainless bolsters, a polished acorn shield and "crackle" mammoth ivory handle scales. *(Jocelyn Frasier Photography)*

STEPHANE SAGRIC: The "Ghost Folder" frequents its favorite haunts in a hand-rubbed satin-finished RWL-34 blade, heat-colored zirconium bolsters and "Blackwood Carbon Fiber" handle scales set on titanium liners. *(BladeGallery.com photo)*

EVAN NICOLAIDES: A no-frills front flipper folder sports a CPM 20CV blade and vintage Paper Micarta handle scales. *(Mitchell D. Cohen Photography)*

FRANCOIS DU TOIT: A front flipper folder exhibits a satin-finished RWL-34 blade, Damasteel bolsters and white TechnoCarbo handle scales set on titanium liners. The folder also features an Ikoma Korth Bearing System (IKBS). *(BladeGallery.com photo)*

WILLIAM ZERMENO: The titanium handle of the CPM 154 folder is milled out to accept FatCarbon handle scales, titanium screws, a pocket clip and lock bar stabilizer. *(Jocelyn Frasier Photography)*

SHANE MAGNUSSEN: With its hand grenade look and feel, the "BBV2" flipper folder pulls duty in a CPM S90V blade, checkered titanium frame and G-10 pivot collars. *(SharpByCoop photo)*

» LUCAS GUMBINER: A full-dress "Omen" flipper folder combines Damasteel, pearl and zirconium. *(Mitchell D. Cohen Photography)*

» BRIAN BROWN: "Custom 51 Blue" is a beauty, featuring a Fafnir Damasteel blade, titanium frame, mosaic mother-of-pearl inlays and a sapphire-inlaid pivot head. *(Mitchell D. Cohen Photography)*

» RIAAN MANSER: A fresh take on folders comes in the form of a keyhole model with a CPM-MagnaCut stainless blade, and a black G-10 handle with FatCarbon "Copper Camo" scales. *(BladeGallery.com photo)*

» LARRY CHEW: The dapper trapper is displayed here in carbon-fiber handle scales and titanium bolsters engraved by Wilfred Valtakis II. *(SharpByCoop photo)*

« BRIAN NADEAU: A sleek flipper folder wears its Damaworks stainless damascus blade and carbon-fiber handle inlay well. *(Jocelyn Frasier Photography)*

« KELLY VERMEER-VELLA: The "Riptide" locking-liner folder is done up in damascus, 24k-gold inlay and fossilized mammoth bone handle scales. *(SharpByCoop photo)*

« BARRY BARNARDT: Soak in the heat-colored Bertie Rietveld "Dragonskin" damascus blade, the "fracture" damascus bolsters and cross-cut carbon-fiber handle scales. *(BladeGallery.com photo)*

KOSIE STEENKAMP: The combination of FatCarbon "Lavaflow" handle scales and carbon-fiber bolsters is truly inspired on a Bohler M390 flipper folder. *(BladeGallery.com photo)*

DARRIEL CASTON: The treatment of the titanium frames and M390 folder blades is what rockets the group into the stratosphere. *(SharpByCoop photo)*

» BRIAN EFROS: A frame-lock folder features a titanium handle with mother-of-pearl underlays, and a black Timascus back spacer and pocket clip. *(Mitchell D. Cohen Photography)*

» RYUICHI "DEW" HARA:
The "Noah Flipper" is a masterpiece built from an M390 stainless blade inlaid with decorative anodized titanium, a finished shipwreck copper handle featuring mother-of-pearl inserts and a ball bearing pivot. *(BladeGallery.com photo)*

TREVOR BURGER:
A nice frame-lock front flipper in Elmax stainless steel features a combination titanium and green canvas Micarta handle. *(BladeGallery.com photo)*

BRIAN FELLHOELTER:
Titanium and MagnaCut steel make up the bulk of the "Ridgeline" auto folder. *(Mitchell D. Cohen Photography)*

» BRYAN MONTALVO:
A "K9 Pup" locking-liner folder features a Vegas Forge M134 barrel damascus blade, gold G-10 handle scales, and zirconium for the rear bolsters, pocket clip, pivot collars and back spacer. *(Mitchell D. Cohen Photography)*

» NICK CHUPRIN:
Starburst patterns dominate the titanium handles of these CPM S45VN prototypes. *(Mitchell D. Cohen Photography)*

MICHAEL WALKER: The stylish BladeLock folder looks great in stainless damascus and gold Mokume/Shakudo (gold and copper). *(Mitchell D. Cohen Photography)*

EYAL LANDESMAN: A tasteful folding dagger features an Odin's Eye Damasteel blade, titanium frame and hardware, mother-of-pearl handle slabs and gold- and black-lip pearl inlays. *(SharpByCoop photo)*

CASEY MIDDLETON: The 22-layer white paper san mai blade is on parade, here accompanied by a hatch-marked handle. *(Mitchell D. Cohen Photography)*

MIKE HAUSER: More than one knife in this chapter has a checkered titanium handle frame, a trend perhaps, but few as beautiful a damascus blade as the auto folder shown here. *(Mitchell D. Cohen Photography)*

TASHI BHARUCHA: A hefty, recurved, hand-ground CPM 154 stainless blade makes up the business end of the "Son of Sam" flipper folder, featuring a marbled carbon-fiber handle. *(BladeGallery.com photo)*

DAVID BEAVER: A fresh flipper folder is accomplished in Chad Nichols' "Mind Melt" mosaic damascus, zirconium bolsters and cross-cut carbon-fiber handle scales. *(SharpByCoop photo)*

DMITRY SINKEVICH: With a san mai blade and 3D-milled titanium handle, the flipper folder also sports inlays of TechnoCarbo and CarboQuartz red dots and a zirconium spine. *(Mitchell D. Cohen Photography)*

HONORÉ VILAIN: The maker couldn't decide on a slip-joint or lockback RWL-34 folder, so he fashioned both: one in vintage rag Micarta and the other with a mammoth ivory grip. *(SharpByCoop photo)*

JAMES BUCKLEY: The handle of the "Predator Spearpoon" (spear-point harpoon blade) frame-lock folder is done in a special titanium oil finish. *(Mitchell D. Cohen Photography)*

HENNIE STEENKAMP: A flipper folder comes to life in a Damasteel "Daupner"-pattern blade, and a titanium handle with Timascus inlays *(BladeGallery.com photo)*

STEFANO COMPOSTELLA: Using two steels—ASP APZ10 Erasteel and "Vinland" Damasteel—the maker accomplished something remarkable. *(SharpByCoop photo)*

DUSTIN DRIVER: The treatment of the crosshatched titanium handle frame and CPM Magnacut blade give the frame-lock folder a stealth look and feel. *(SharpByCoop photo)*

D.R. DAVIS: The "Eclipse" slip-joint folder displays a Doug Ponzio mosaic damascus blade, an integral titanium frame, mother-of-pearl inlays and gold screws for good measure. *(Mitchell D. Cohen Photography)*

KIRBY LAMBERT: An "Augustus" flipper folder is delivered in a W2 blade with hamon (temper line), carbon-fiber handle scales and zirconium bolsters. *(Mitchell D. Cohen Photography)*

JEREMY MARSH: The maker's "Maelstrom" flipper features Westinghouse Micarta over a titanium frame. *(Mitchell D. Cohen Photography)*

KIRK MARBERRY: Mother-of-pearl and carbon fiber are a rare pairing, discovered here on a spear-point flipper folder. *(Mitchell D. Cohen Photography)*

HERUCUS BLOMERUS: An HB16 flipper integrates unidirectional FatCarbon handle scales, zirconium bolsters and an M390 stainless blade. *(BladeGallery.com photo)*

ANDREW DEMKO: The dimpled titanium handle of the Magnacut folder gives it a fresh look and feel. *(SharpByCoop photo)*

JOHN GRAY: Equally impressive are the milled and anodized titanium frame and "Darkrain"-finished blade. *(Mitchell D. Cohen Photography)*

EDWARD RATANUN: The maker builds one in a "Grabak" Damasteel blade, twist-damascus bolsters and black glass Westinghouse Micarta handle scales. *(Mitchell D. Cohen Photography)*

JEREMY KRAMMES: The curvaceous flipper folder incorporates a Chad Nichols san mai blade, zirconium bolsters and ivory G-10 handle inserts. *(SharpByCoop photo)*

DANIEL KEOWN: Okay, now, we've got a "Big City Fighter" AEB-L folding knife in stainless hardware with mammoth ivory handle scales. *(SharpByCoop photo)*

BARRET CHRISMAN: He was dealt a Damasteel and titanium hand, and, man, did he make the best of it! (SharpByCoop photo)

STEVE HILL: The scarred, heat-colored heart on each side of the wave-pattern damascus blade of the mammoth ivory-handle folder represents the maker's recovery from a heart attack.

BRIAN BIEGLER: The "Kuma" butterfly knife arrives in a W2 blade with wispy temper line and leather-wrapped anodized titanium handle halves. *(SharpByCoop photo)*

LUCAS BURNLEY: The maker's M-69 model arrives in Damasteel and jade-anodized, deep laser-engraved titanium. *(SharpByCoop photo)*

ERIC TUCH: Double red CarboQuartz inlays within black paper Micarta handle scales complement a rose damascus blade. *(Mitchell D. Cohen Photography)*

» **CHRIS RICHARDSON:** The silver and enamel artwork is framed in zirconium on a twist-damascus folder. *(SharpByCoop photo)*

« **DANIEL KOERT:** "Micro John" looks dapper in emerald-green Micarta, Hakkapella Damasteel damascus and zirconium. *(Mitchell D. Cohen Photography)*

« **JAVIER VOGT:** In the auto-folding dagger realm is a tightly patterned damascus beauty in stag handle scales and golden engraving. *(SharpByCoop photo)*

» **IAN PICKARSKI:** The Balisong folder integrates titanium handle halves with mother-of-pearl underlays. *(Mitchell D. Cohen Photography)*

« **SCOTT GALLAGHER:** Mosaic damascus patterning flows from the blade to the bolsters and lands softly on a bed of fossil walrus ivory. *(Jocelyn Frasier Photography)*

» **JONATHAN MCNEES:** The "PM Mac 2" sports a 3.5-inch drop-point blade and a "frag"-pattern handle based on fragmentation devices from World War II, such as the MK2 pineapple grenade. *(Mitchell D. Cohen Photography)*

Take-Down Knives

Imagine if modern car manufacturers not only made models that could be taken apart, but marketed them as such, or if kitchen appliance dealers delivered "take-down" dishwashers or take-apart refrigerators and microwave ovens. Honestly, it doesn't matter—they wouldn't be as cool as take-down knives anyway, at least not handmade, finely fit and finished custom blades with tools to unscrew tangs from pommels, allowing handles to slide off and entire assemblies to be disassembled.

Such are the offerings of a small but growing legion of knifemakers who wanted to show collectors, users and enthusiasts how their knives are assembled, and to provide the means to take them apart and put them back together again. Ah, genius, and when reassembled, the blades don't wiggle, there are no gaps in the guards, and the handles are tight, palpable and proportional.

And, since such highly skilled knifemakers fashion all parts of their knives, the disassembly tools are handmade as well, making take-down knives coveted collector items that are meant to be used, taken apart, reassembled and admired.

» **QUINTIN T. HARDTNER:** You can disassemble and reassemble the feather-damascus bowie with fossil walrus tusk handle as often as you like. *(SharpByCoop photo)*

JOSH HULTS:
The integral damascus hunter can be taken apart via the pommel nut at the end of the redwood handle. *(Jocelyn Frasier Photography)*

JACCO VAN DE BRUINHORST: Using the little tool at right, one can take down the bowie with a floral mosaic-pattern damascus blade and desert ironwood grip to see what makes it so special. *(SharpByCoop photo)*

Persian Versions

BRIAN SELLERS: The flowing lines of a Persian fighter are accomplished in ladder-pattern damascus, silver and African blackwood. *(Jocelyn Frasier Photography)*

D.R. DAVIS: A little Persian flair lends sweeping beauty to a blued damascus slip-joint folder with a lightning-etched titanium frame and mother-of-pearl handle inserts. *(Mitchell D. Cohen Photography)*

» **LLOYD HALE and LARRY HIRSCH:** The 440C Persian fighter dons an imitation tortoise shell handle and nickel silver liners. *(SharpByCoop photo)*

JESS HOFFMAN: The maker's "Tenbruchs 85" is a Persian-influenced, flat-ground 52100 skinner with a sweeping blade and Wenge wood handle. (*Jocelyn Frasier Photography)*

» **JOHN HORRIGAN:**
A pretty Persian fighter takes advantage of a twist-damascus blade, ebony handle, and 24k-gold leaf and vine overlays. (*Mitchell D. Cohen Photography*)

« **BERTIE RIETVELD:**
A solid Persian-style integral art knife is done up in "Dragonskin" damascus, black jade inlays and a stanhope lens in front of the handle. (*SharpByCoop photo*)

Ripped Fighters

When fighters like these enter the ring, there's a lot to live up to—those who've come before and served in wars; others that have been used for self-defense; in emergency situations such as to jimmy a lock, cut a seatbelt or clothing or bust a hinge; and for piercing, slashing, and like their human brethren, upper cutting.

So, one thinks, how hard can it be to repeat patterns executed for millennia? That's like asking an actor if it was easy portraying a historic figure, or a mom if it was simple to raise children after the examples of Abigail Adams, Alberta King or the fictional June Cleaver.

It's almost more difficult to perfect what has been tried and tested than it is to create something new altogether. The main problem is getting something right that has proven effective in the past. One wrong measurement or pin placement and the balance is skewed or the aesthetics ruined. When there are few embellishments, bells and whistles, there's less room for error. The perfection of a pretty face is skin-deep beauty, but the execution of ripped fighters takes internal integrity, guts and polished practices.

« AARON BIEBER: A Kwaiken-inspired adventure is completed in AEB-L steel and desert ironwood. *(SharpByCoop photo)*

» JON MOORE: This mittful of a model comes in a sweet hand-forged, canned damascus blade, a fighter-style Bocote wood handle, stainless "S-guard" and a leather belt sheath with rattlesnake skin inlays.

» MAL HANNAN:
A recurved 440C blade makes up 8 of the 15 inches on a fighter, with the other 7 inches being a stabilized York gum burl handle. *(Rod Hoare photo)*

» RYAN BREUER:
A recurved 80CrV2 fighter stands tall in a blued damascus guard and ironwood grip. *(SharpByCoop photo)*

» DEON NEL:
A ripped fighter comes out swinging in Hakkapella Damasteel and ivory paper Micarta. *(Mitchell D. Cohen Photography)*

« CHRIS ROOSENDAAL: The integral damascus fighter is a doozy, here in a big leaf maple handle, and copper and G-10 spacers. *(Rod Hoare photo)*

« MICHAEL HOBBS: The "Genesis" is born from 449-layer random-pattern san mai damascus, Dark Matter carbon fiber, red G-10 and curly Siamese rosewood. *(SharpByCoop photo)*

« JERRY HOSSOM: The "Large Narc Fighter" wears a CTS-XHP blade, Richlite handle and devilish smile. *(Mitchell D. Cohen Photography)*

» LUKE DELLMYER: The 80CrV2 model with blued guard and Tazmanian blackwood handle is an award winner and part of the maker's set of American Bladesmith Society journeyman smith knives. *(SharpByCoop photo)*

» JOSH FISHER: You can follow the lines of the fine fighter from its hand-checkered ringed Gidgee wood handle all the way to the tip of the feathery damascus blade. *(Jocelyn Frasier Photography)*

» BOB APPLEBY: A Bob Loveless-style fighter finds its rhythm in CPM 154 steel, 416 stainless and amber-dyed sambar stag. *(SharpByCoop photo)*

« TRAVIS FRY:
A coffin-handle fighter leads with its flat-ground W2 blade and comes back swinging in a curly Yarran (acacia wood) grip and brass liners. *(Jocelyn Frasier Photography)*

« MICHAEL DALY:
The hollow-ground recurved tactical comes calling in black paper Micarta, red linen liners and a CPM 154 steel blade. *(SharpByCoop photo)*

« PHIL EVANS:
A 5160 fighter is adorned in blued mild steel fittings, stainless liners and ironwood handle scales. *(Jocelyn Frasier Photography)*

LONNIE JENSEN: The "Sidekick" comes at you in a black 80CrV2 blade, checkered carbon-fiber handle and a Jeremy Jensen "Red Bear" Kydex sheath. *(SharpByCoop photo)*

JOHN SCHULTZ: Twist damascus and ironwood are the one-two punch of a fighter. *(Mitchell D. Cohen Photography)*

STEVEN RAMOS: The ripped CPM 154 fighter with fancy gemstone handle is hollow ground and a handful. *(SharpByCoop photo)*

BROCK WOODSON: "Ghost in my Death" intimidates its victims via a Cu Mai blade with oil slick finish. *(Mitchell D. Cohen Photography)*

SETH LOPEZ: Relish the fully integral, recurved fighter in a damascus blade, African blackwood handle and domed stainless pins. *(SharpByCoop photo)*

PAUL SARGANIS: A KA-BAR/Bob Loveless "Dixon"-style fighter is executed in an AEB-L stainless blade, a black Micarta guard and pommel, and stacked natural Micarta handle spacers with fluted black Micarta spacers in between. *(BladeGallery.com photo)*

KELLY VERMEER-VELLA: The "Stormtrooper" fighter is fashioned with a Koa wood handle and that swell "Flying Ws" damascus blade. *(SharpByCoop photo)*

Classically Styled

» **MATT PARKINSON:** The "Medieval Knife" makes good use of modern silver fittings and a Koa wood handle. *(SharpByCoop photo)*

ANDERS HOGSTROM: The Quetzalcoatl Aztec ceremonial dagger dresses for the part in a 5.5-inch blade with double hamon (temper line), bronze fittings and a blackwood and fossil walrus ivory handle. *(Mitchell D. Cohen Photography)*

CHARLIE ELLIS: A forged tanto shows a smoky temper line and is highlighted by an Osage orange wood handle with nylon cord wrap. *(BladeGallery.com photo)*

BRENDAN ATKINSON: The maker's version of a wakizashi is accomplished in she oak, copper and Nitro V stainless steel. *(Rod Hoare photo)*

» DAVID MIRABILE:
A Japanese dragonfly-style blade is forged from W2 tool steel and accompanied by a molded carbon-fiber bolster, handle, and ito (handle wrap) and ancient walrus ivory pommel.
(SharpByCoop photo)

LIN RHEA:
A beautifully rendered Puukko parades a stacked ironwood, Micarta and antler handle and comes with a Josh Rhea sheath. *(Jocelyn Frasier Photography)*

» KEVIN HARVEY:
A California-style dagger exhibits a hand-forged and heat-treated twist-damascus blade, engraved nickel silver bolster and ferrule and African wattle burl handle scales.
(BladeGallery.com photo)

RANDY CASTON:
"Bowie #1" imagines the first such piece in a 1075 blade, sterling silver guard and pins, and a walnut burl handle.
(SharpByCoop photo)

ROBERT YOUNG: A "New York Special Flipper" takes Bob Loveless styling to new levels, including an RWL-34 blade, stainless liners, stag handle scales and ceramic bearings. *(Jocelyn Frasier Photography)*

PAUL SARGANIS: One boot knife in the style of Bob Loveless sports a satin-finished AEB-L stainless blade and stag handle scales. *(BladeGallery.com photo)*

GABRIEL TURNER: A seax looks dapper in damascus, wrought iron and wood. *(SharpByCoop photo)*

CARL MICHAEL ALMQVIST: A Swedish hunter parades a Kent Andersson damascus blade, stabilized curly birch handle and hand-engraved reindeer antler bolsters. *(BladeGallery.com photo)*

» PATRICK HARP:
Say hello to the Samuel Bell-style bowie begotten from 240-layer damascus, mammoth ivory and wrought iron. *(SharpByCoop photo)*

« DON HANSON III:
The maker's version of a Remington bullet knife incorporates W2 tool steel and ancient ivory.
(Mitchell D. Cohen Photography)

» MARDI MESHEJIAN:
A fine example of a Tanto Shirasaya features an upswept, flat-ground damascus blade, and a bloodwood handle and saya (sheath).
(SharpByCoop photo)

^ J.W. RANDALL:
A Michael Price-style California dagger exhibits a ladder-pattern damascus blade, African ebony handle and gold-lip pearl inlays.
(Jocelyn Frasier Photography)

» JAVIER VOGT:
The classic part stops at the styling of the tanto, and everything else, including it being a guard-release auto-folder with a san mai blade, hot-blued guard, and carved carbon-fiber handle having stingray skin inserts, is modern.
(SharpByCoop photo)

« J.J. SIMON:
A Samuel Bell-style dirk has a bloomery steel blade, an engraved nickel silver guard and pommel and a blackwood handle with silver pins.
(SharpByCoop photo)

» BEN SEWARD:
A traditional hand-forged damascus Kwaiken exhibits a cord-wrapped natural Micarta handle and comes with a felt-lined Kydex sheath.
(BladeGallery.com photo)

JASON CHEN:
For this dog bone bowie with desert ironwood grip and domed pines that emulates an antique L. Kimball knife, the maker took home the Joe Keeslar Award at the 2024 BLADE Show for the best knife submitted by a successful journeyman smith.
(SharpByCoop photo)

» EDDIE RAY: A Bob Loveless whittler pattern sports a Westinghouse paper Micarta handle, ATS-34 blade and stainless guard engraved by Alice Carter. *(Mitchell D. Cohen Photography)*

JACCO VAN DE BRUINHORST: A pair of mosaic damascus San Francisco-style gent's knives arrive in mosaic damascus and mother-of-pearl handles, sculpted pommels and silver sheaths engraved by Wolfgang Loerchner. *(SharpByCoop photo)*

« COLOTON ARIAS: The maker's take on an Etruscan Bronze Age dagger includes a "triple feather" mosaic damascus blade, mild steel and brass accents, and a goat leather-wrapped handle. *(Jocelyn Frasier Photography)*

SAMUEL LURQUIN: A splendid example of a Musso bowie (like that once owned by Joe Musso and eventually donated to The Alamo) features a damascus guard and African blackwood handle. *(SharpByCoop photo)*

» ADAM GRAY: The "Micro Bushcrafter" pays homage to the style, here in a CPM 154 steel blade, Wenge wood handle scales and G-10 liners. *(Jocelyn Frasier Photography)*

SCHUYLER LOVESTRAND: A Loveless Big Bear is brought to life in CPM 154 steel, stainless and amber stag. *(SharpByCoop photo)*

» MACE VITALE: Inspired by an 1850 Otto & Koehler fixed blade, the W2 beauty boasts a carved mammoth ivory handle and nickel silver furniture. *(Mitchell D. Cohen Photography)*

« CHUCK COOK: A classic seax is accomplished in a 7.75-inch damascus blade, carbon-fiber frame and stabilized maple handle. *(SharpByCoop photo)*

» STEVEN BRYAN: Based on a machete found on the face of a volcano in rural Guatemala, the maker's version is forged in high-layer damascus and handled in curly maple. *(SharpByCoop photo)*

« KARIS FISHER: Modeled after an antique bowie, the maker's version is rendered in 52100 steel and a checkered African blackwood handle with stainless fittings. *(Mitchell D. Cohen Photography)*

» NATE "TUNA" GRANT: The "Maguro Bocho" is a classic Japanese tuna knife, in this case featuring a long 80CrV2 blade, brass guard, and a brass, G-10 and Osage orange handle. *(SharpByCoop photo)*

GARY MARTINDALE: A Bob Loveless-style chute knife is executed in CPM 154 and stainless steels, red liners and amber stag handle scales. *(SharpByCoop photo)*

Super Synthetics

Lightning Strike carbon fiber, G-Carta, G-10, Kenobi-Ti, and every type of vintage butterscotch, emerald-green, ivory and otherwise gorgeous Westinghouse Micarta one can lay their hands on—these are the Super Synthetics of the modern era, and knife lovers, collectors and all-around users are gobbling them up as fast as the manufacturers can pump out such modern materials.

The list doesn't stop there. Moku-Ti, zirco-ti, Timascus, marbled carbon fiber, FatCarbon, Richlite, Raffir, TeroTuf, exotic resins, resin acrylics, Voodoo Resins and "glow synthetics" are here to light up our lives. And they're stable, don't shrink, crack, buckle or break.

Are they aesthetically superior to wood, pearl, ivory or stone? Can they outshine natural materials or replace what Mother Nature has created? Perhaps the idea isn't which is better, more beautiful or alluring, but instead how one complements the other. Taken together, knifemakers and users alike have choices and variety, and in that case, it's likely that super synthetics have forged their own lane and are here to stay.

DAVID HALL: Mint-green and burnt-orange G-10 highlights the 1084-and-15N20 damascus camp knife. *(Mitchell D. Cohen Photography)*

ANDREW DEMKO: It took a long, beefy titanium handle frame to counterbalance the 6-inch Magnacut blade of a tactical folder with Shark-Lock. *(SharpByCoop photo)*

» MATT DAVIS:
Black Micarta handle scales hug the full tang of a stainless EDC fixed blade in a trademarked "The Davis Grind." *(Jocelyn Frasier Photography)*

» CHARLIE ELLIS:
Hand-forged damascus and black paper Richlite give the drop-point hunter a dark demeanor.
(BladeGallery.com photo)

» MAL HANNAN:
Canvas Micarta gets equal billing on a tactical knife along with a bead-blasted D2 blade. *(Rod Hoare photo)*

« SERGE PANCHENKO:
The "Rook" is a collaboration with Wilfred Vallakis, who engraved, anodized and enhanced the folder with tritium.
(Mitchell D. Cohen Photography)

» ULYSSE ROBERT: Westinghouse Micarta handle scales sandwich the titanium frame of a "Dryad" folder, here in W2 tool steel. *(Jocelyn Frasier Photography)*

« MICHAEL WALKER: A "Bolstered D-Lock" is tastefully executed in stainless damascus and tinted titanium. *(SharpByCoop photo)*

» STEPHANE ESPI: Burgundy paper Micarta handle scales make a guy want to sit down with the damascus front flipper folder and a nice glass of wine. *(BladeGallery.com photo)*

CHRISTIAN HOLM: The "Draugr MKIII" military knife enlists a flat saber-ground 80CrV2 blade in a black Cerakote finish and an olive-green G-10 handle. *(Rod Hoare photo)*

JERRY HOSSOM: "Reprisal" in this case takes the form of a feather damascus blade and a Juma snakeskin resin-based handle. *(Mitchell D. Cohen Photography)*

FRANCOIS DU TOIT: The RWL-34 front flipper is outfitted with a FatCarbon "Lava Flow" handle that looks every bit of the part. *(BladeGallery.com photo)*

JAMIE BISHOP: Paper Micarta adds a splash of color to a beautiful stainless damascus Gyuto chef's knife. *(Rod Hoare photo)*

JOHN C. THUNERT: A flat-ground damascus drop-point fixed-blade sashays "Prickly Pear Skeleton Crazy" fiber handle scales and G-10 liners. *(Jocelyn Frasier Photography)*

» COLLIN MAGUIRE:
Those are FatCarbon "Polar White Dark Matter" handle scales on the otherwise all-damascus fixed blade, including a four-bar "Firestorm" and feather-pattern blade. *(SharpByCoop photo)*

« RICHARD SOLER:
A front flipper folder features a World War II-era rag Micarta handle and a stonewashed RWL-34 blade. *(BladeGallery.com photo)*

» DAVID JESSIE II:
The "Hellbender" gets right down to business in CPM S30V steel and canvas Micarta. *(Mitchell D. Cohen Photography)*

« JOSHUA FISHER:
Teal burlap Micarta gets top billing on a full-tang Nitro-V stainless Kwaiken model. *(BladeGallery.com photo)*

» DAVID TABER:
A CPM-154 lockback whittler is clad in CarboQuartz handle scales. *(SharpByCoop photo)*

JESS HOFFMAN:
Check out the satin-finished, hollow-ground AEB-L blade of the "Tipperary," and that Westinghouse canvas Micarta handle. *(Jocelyn Frasier Photography)*

» KYLE HANSON:
The tapered-tang fixed blade exhibits keen W2 steel with a smoky temper line and a sculpted Micarta handle. *(Mitchell D. Cohen Photography)*

ERIK FRITZ:
A 5.5-inch stainless utility slicer is outfitted with attractive Kirinite handle scales set on a full tang. *(BladeGallery.com photo))*

JOSH HULTS:
Brilliant G-carta handle scales put some G-forces behind the 4.5-inch 1085 fixed blade. *(Jocelyn Frasier Photography)*

PAUL KILBY:
Crackled Ultem (thermoplastic) makes up the gorgeous handle half of an AEB-L flipper folder. *(Mitchell D. Cohen Photography)*

CURTIS HAALAND:
"The Outpost" enters the fray in a 52100 high-carbon steel blade with a black oxide finish, a hand-sculpted vintage linen Micarta handle and black G-10 bolsters. *(BladeGallery.com photo)*

BRIAN NADEAU:
The "Tempest" stirs up a storm via its Vegas Forge "Reptilian" damascus blade and grooved zirconium handle scales. *(Jocelyn Frasier Photography)*

NICK MARSHALL: The "Wren" folder takes flight in a "Hornet's Nest" damascus blade, and a handle with black glass Durostone and vintage emerald-green Micarta inlays. *(Mitchell D. Cohen Photography)*

RYUICHI "DEW" HARA: FatCarbon "Lava Flow" handle scales help enliven the M390 stainless flipper folder along with "Kintsugi Raden" inlays. *(BladeGallery.com photo)*

GAVIN HAWK: FatCarbon handle inlays and a blackened blade highlight the "Deadlock" out-the-front folder. *(Mitchell D. Cohen Photography)*

NEELS ROOS: An engraved "Neptune" front flipper folder hits the market in a hand-ground Damasteel blade and FatCarbon "Toxic Storm" handle. *(BladeGallery.com photo)*

» ERIC TUCH: The sculpted titanium handle scales of an RWL-34 folder feature vintage Westinghouse Micarta inlays and black Timascus accents. *(Mitchell D. Cohen Photography)*

« STEPHANE SAGRIC: The "Snipper" front flipper LinerLock is let loose in FatCarbon "Arctic Storm" handle scales, heat-colored zirconium bolsters and an RWL-34 blade. *(BladeGallery.com photo)*

» BILL RUPLE: The maker outfits his drop-point hunter with a vintage rag Micarta handle and Westinghouse Micarta shield. *(Mitchell D. Cohen Photography)*

« LUCAS BURNLEY: Burgundy canvas Micarta provides hand purchase for an integral Kihoku AEB-l steel model. *(SharpByCoop photo)*

» PATRICK FAMIN: A sleek out-the-front dual-action auto sports a san mai blade, an aluminum handle frame with vintage Westinghouse Micarta overlays and zirconium bolsters. *(Mitchell D. Cohen Photography)*

» KOSIE STEENKAMP: Red Coral canvas-Micarta handle scales and vintage natural Micarta bolsters are a nod to tradition on an otherwise modern front flipper folder with a Bohler M390 stainless blade. *(BladeGallery.com photo)*

» BOBBY HOUSE: Bobby fashions a Barlow in a Vegas Forge "Virus" damascus blade and a two-tone Micarta handle. *(Mitchell D. Cohen Photography)*

JOHN D. CHAPMAN: A FatCarbon handle with carbon-fiber guard makes for a cool combination on an AEB-L drop-point hunter. *(SharpByCoop photo)*

» JEFF VANDERMEULEN: The folding cleaver sports a Magnacut CPM blade, titanium frame and "Arctic Storm" FatCarbon handle scales. *(Mitchell D. Cohen Photography)*

» TASHI BHARUCHA: The "Die Hard Flipper" is delivered in a Sam Lurquin "Laddered Ws"-pattern damascus blade, copper niobium superconductor bolsters and FatCarbon "Copper Space Coral" handle scales. *(BladeGallery.com photo)*

» KIRK MARBERRY: The super synthetic handle materials of a Wharncliffe flipper folder include marbled carbon fiber, and white and "Tiffany blue" G-10. *(Mitchell D. Cohen Photography)*

« TOM BULLOCK: As if the Cu-Mai blade wasn't enough, the "Lanny's clip"-style folder is presented in phenolic handle scales from an antique bowling ball. *(BladeGallery.com photo)*

» BRANDON CORBIN: Emerald Micarta handle scales play their part on a "Mini Lanza" folder featuring a Mike Norris "Fireclone 2" damascus blade, zirconium bolsters and a black-lip pearl pivot head and underlay. *(Mitchell D. Cohen Photography)*

» JACOB PETERSON: The "AdventureCraft Brick" edition is dominated by a colorful chromium trioxide and alumina handle and a gold CPM S35VN blade. *(Mitchell D. Cohen Photography)*

» EVAN NICOLAIDES: The "COBIA" folder enrolls a CPM 20CV blade and a blue Richlite and titanium handle. *(Mitchell D. Cohen Photography)*

DAVID BEAVER: The sweeping "Horizon" is picturesque in a Bjorkman's Twist Damasteel blade, Aletai meteorite bolsters and vintage emerald-green Micarta handle scales. *(SharpByCoop photo)*

» JEREMY MARSH: Mind-blowing materials of the "California Vanquish" model include Damasteel (blade), Superconductor (bolsters) and Westinghouse Micarta (handle). *(Mitchell D. Cohen Photography)*

« BRIAN EFROS: "Broadway Jr." is a star in the making, dressed for success in a Damasteel blade, Westinghouse Micarta handle scales and Timascus liners. *(Mitchell D. Cohen Photography)*

» HERUCUS BLOMERUS: Between the "Grabak" Damasteel blade and bolsters, and Chad Nichols Kenobi-Ti handle scales, the flipper folder is a fox. *(SharpByCoop photo)*

« LUKE SWENSON: The modified hawkbill folder is fashioned using a CPM 154 stainless blade and vintage blue and beige linen Micarta handle scales. *(Mitchell D. Cohen Photography)*

K.C. GRAY: The "Hony Creeper" LinerLock features a 4-inch Chad Nichols "Turkish Twist" damascus blade, red paper Micarta handle scales, carbon-fiber bolsters, jeweled titanium liners, and a Timascus back spacer, pivot collars and screws. *(Mitchell D. Cohen Photography)*

BRYAN MONTALVO: "Akita" stands at attention in a damascus blade, World War II-era rag Micarta handle scales and resin "Fight Club" Micarta bolsters. *(Mitchell D. Cohen Photography)*

BARRET CHRISMAN: Vintage butterscotch Micarta is the super synthetic handle material of a folding pocketknife with Bertie Rietveld "Fracture" damascus blade. I just like the surfboard shield. *(SharpByCoop photo)*

KYLE DAILY: A 7-inch Santoku is outfitted in a CPM 154 blade, "Red Firehose" Micarta handle scales, brown canvas Micarta and white G-10 liners and Micarta pins. *(Mitchell D. Cohen Photography)*

» ARNO BERNARD: Among other amenities, a frame-lock flipper folder sports a Bohler M390 stainless blade, titanium frame and blue TechnoCarbo inlays. *(BladeGallery.com photo)*

» CARLOS QUEIROS: The carbon-fiber composite handle of the RWL-34 "Toxicity" folder is anything but toxic. *(Mitchell D. Cohen Photography)*

» TREVOR BURGER: Green Micarta handle scales pull duty on an EXK 30 slip joint in an Elmax stainless blade. *(BladeGallery.com photo)*

JASON KNIGHT: The 80CrV2 "Fett Camp Knife" practically glows via the G-10 handle with opal G-10 liners/underlays. *(SharpByCoop photo)*

» CASEY MIDDLETON:
The "Chupacabra" model parades a vintage Westinghouse Micarta handle and Baker Forge san mai steel blade. *(Mitchell D. Cohen Photography)*

RIAAN MANSER:
A black G-10 handle frame outlines the FatCarbon "Raindrop Copper" inlays of a CPM MagnaCut stainless flipper folder. *(BladeGallery.com photo)*

» CHARLIE LLOYD:
The "Osprey" flipper sports a 416 stainless-nickel-and-1080 san mai blade, and vintage butterscotch Micarta handle scales. *(SharpByCoop photo)*

DANIEL KOERT:
The "Mini Sabot" is dressed to the nines in vintage blue Micarta, Mike Norris san mai damascus and mother-of-pearl. *(Mitchell D. Cohen Photography)*

CORRIE SCHOEMAN: The "Snout" front flipper is fashioned from a Pieter Goosen damascus blade, caged bearings and black G-10 handle scales with Raffir Noble copper mesh overlays. *(BladeGallery.com photo)*

LEIGH CANTWELL: While the acid-etched 15N20 high-carbon steel blade is the star of the rare "Bam Bam" art kitchen knife, the yellow G-10 handle scales and carbon-fiber pins have their place. *(Rod Hoare photo)*

CHARLES GEDRAITIS: Inspired by Luke Skywalker, the Swiss Army switchblade features titanium handle scales with bronze and carbon-fiber inlays, and blue ice DayGlo G-10 inserts. *(Mitchell D. Cohen Photography)*

Bird & Trout Knives

» JONATHAN CARUSO:
The mild steel collar and buttcap of a stag-handle 1075 bird & trout knife are torched blue like a lake teeming with fish. *(Jocelyn Frasier Photography)*

» DAVID KELLEY:
A CPM 154 "Fin and Feather" model features an amber jigged bone handle, tapered tang and natural canvas Micarta liners.
(Mitchell D. Cohen Photography)

» CRAIG BROSMAN:
The bird & trout knife is a breath of fresh air, here in an amber European red stag handle and CPM 154 blade.
(SharpByCoop photo)

« GABRIEL MABRY:
While the black ash burl handle of a bird & trout knife is dyed and stabilized, its 80CrV2 carbon steel blade displays an antique finish.
(BladeGallery.com photo)

PAUL KILBY:
Stag and AEB-L steel share billing on a bird & trout knife.
(Mitchell D. Cohen Photography)

Best-in-Class Bowies

» JESSE HU: "Explosion" and "X-Recursion" patterns of mosaic damascus take center stage on a pair of bowies in ringed Gidgee and curly Koa wood handles. *(Jocelyn Frasier Photography)*

» ANDREAS KALANI: The "Heritage" bowie features a high-carbon steel blade with smoky temper line, a sambar stag handle, a brass guard and pommel engraved in a damascus pattern and leather spacers.

« TOMMY GANN: A frame-handle bowie looks regal in a hand-forged, satin-finished 52100 blade, a nickel silver guard and stabilized curly Koa handle. *(BladeGallery.com photo)*

» **RON SUTTON:**
Vasticola burl meets a 608-layer random-pattern damascus blade at the mild steel guard of a clip-point bowie. (*Rod Hoare photo*)

» **MACE VITALE:**
The coffin-handle bowie is just menacing enough in W2 tool steel, silver and blackwood.
(*SharpByCoop photo*)

» **CHRIS GARDNER:**
The 16-inch recurved 5160 bowie is anchored by a black and white ebony handle and a 416 stainless guard.
(*Jocelyn Frasier Photography*)

KEVIN HARVEY:
The temper line is clearly visible where the Japanese clay zone heat treatment was applied to a dog bone bowie with a ringed Gidgee handle and nickel silver fittings. (*BladeGallery.com photo*)

» **JAYMES STEVENS:**
The "Totality Bowie" boasts a 1075 blade with smoky hamon (temper line), a nickel silver guard and desert ironwood handle.
(Jocelyn Frasier Photography)

ANDREW BLOMFIELD:
Dazzling is the damascus bowie in blued steel and ringed Gidgee wood.
(SharpByCoop photo)

GARY RODEWALD:
The maker fashions an English-style bowie from a "Laddered Ws" damascus blade, African blackwood handle and stainless guard. *(BladeGallery.com photo)*

SHAWN CROCOS:
A full flat-ground 1084 bowie blends a stainless guard with a desert ironwood handle.
(Rod Hoare photo)

ROB LOGAN:
A gent's bowie blends a dyed and stabilized redwood lace burl handle with musk ox, nickel silver spacers, and a 192-layer damascus blade. *(Jocelyn Frasier Photography)*

BEN SEWARD:
An example of a best-in-class bowie might be one with a damascus blade, satin-finished stainless guard and checkered walnut handle. *(BladeGallery.com photo)*

BRUCE BARNETT:
Stretching nearly 16 inches long overall, the impressive bowie sports a "Twisted Ws" damascus blade and a musk ox horn handle. *(Rod Hoare photo)*

JONATHAN CARUSO:
A flame hamon lends character to the 1095 blade of a stag-handle bowie with a mild steel collar and buttcap. *(Jocelyn Frasier Photography)*

» **BUTCH SHEELY:**
Butch bangs one out in 1080-and-15N20 damascus steel, walrus ivory and nickel silver. *(Mitchell D. Cohen Photography)*

« **MICHAEL ANDERSSON:**
Warning: You may become smitten with the multi-bar damascus bowie, combining a carbon steel central bar and an "explosion"-pattern damascus edge and spine, a stainless guard, reindeer antler handle and damascus frame. *(BladeGallery.com photo)*

» **ED FOWLER:**
Named for American scout and frontiersman Lewis "Deathwind" Wetzel, the bowie is accomplished in a 6.5-inch 52100 blade, brass guard and a 20-year-old black sheep horn handle. *(Jocelyn Frasier Photography)*

« **SHAWN MCINTYRE:**
The damascus "Midnight Blue Bowie" is named for its dyed Tasmanian blackwood handle. (*Rod Hoare photo)*

» CRISTIAN SILVA: A hand-forged damascus bowie is equipped with a gun-blued guard and a sculpted African blackwood handle. *(BladeGallery.com photo)*

« DAWSON TABONE: A classic burl-handle bowie blends a 1075 high-carbon steel blade and a stainless guard. *(Jocelyn Frasier Photography)*

« MATTHEW PARKINSON: A sleek bowie is born from 1084 steel, bronze, maple and the mind of the maker. *(Mitchell D. Cohen Photography)*

« GREGORY CIMDON PENNY: A curvaceous bowie blends a 4-bar "Turkish Twist" damascus blade with a blued mild steel guard and pommel, European red stag handle and walrus ivory spacer. *(Jocelyn Frasier Photography)*

» SAM HEATH: The damascus patterning of a 7.5-inch flat-ground bowie bounces in all the right places and is a nice contrast to the stainless guard and deer antler handle. *(Rod Hoare photo)*

» DUSTIN PARSONS: A red oak burl coffin-handle bowie is brought to fruition in "Crushed Ws" damascus and a clamshell S-guard. *(Jocelyn Frasier Photography)*

» SILVANA MOUZINHO: An exceptional bowie from the Brazilian knifemaker parades a hand-forged 5160 high-carbon steel blade, a satin-finished stainless guard and an Aroeira wood handle. *(BladeGallery.com photo)*

» BILL MILLER: It took a full 15 inches to fit in the "Ws"-pattern damascus blade, nickel silver fittings, sambar stag handle and engraving by Andrew Adams. *(Jocelyn Frasier Photography)*

» KELLY VERMEER-VELLA: The mammoth ivory-handle bowie blends a "Riptide" damascus blade with a twist-damascus frame, and damascus and titanium spacers. *(Mitchell D. Cohen Photography)*

» BOB EARHART: A bowie enjoys the best of both worlds—a mammoth ivory handle and feather damascus blade. *(Jocelyn Frasier Photography)*

« STUART SMITH: The clip-point bowie comes complete with a tight "Ws"-pattern damascus blade, stainless clamshell guard and stabilized curly Koa handle. *(BladeGallery.com photo)*

« JAMES CROWELL: Canister ball bearing damascus ushers in the 10-inch bowie featuring heat-blued 1018 fittings and a stag handle. *(Jocelyn Frasier Photography)*

On-Point Hunters

» **SHAYNE CARTER:** Two Koa-handle "Raindrop Ws" damascus hunters are way better than one. *(SharpByCoop photo)*

CLARENCE DEYONG: If making a drop-point hunter, one might consider a sculpted twist-damascus blade and stag handle. *(Mitchell D. Cohen Photography)*

« **CHAD J. JONES:** One hot hunter showcases a Mike Norris "Hornet's Nest" stainless damascus blade, "Zebra" carbon-fiber bolsters and a cross-cut mammoth tusk handle. *(Jocelyn Frasier Photography)*

« RICHARD KEMP: A well-rounded hunter uses a 26C3 blade, miniritchie wood handle and red G-10 liners to its advantage. *(Rod Hoare photo)*

» WILL DUTTON: Sometimes you need a hand-forged 1084 hunter in a stag handle with natural Micarta spacers and a tooled leather custom pouch sheath (not shown). *(BladeGallery.com photo)*

» PEKKA TUOMINEN: The 6-inch damascus blade of the hunter is just as sweet as the pure silver guard and desert ironwood grip. *(SharpByCoop photo)*

» JASON COY:
A classic clip-point hunter is handled in walnut, outfitted in bronze and copper and bladed in 80CrV2 steel. *(Jocelyn Frasier Photography)*

FRANCOIS MAZIERES:
A hidden-tang drop-point hunter comes to fruition in a hand-forged, differentially heat-treated 1075 blade, sculpted stainless guard and curly silky oak handle. *(Rod Hoare photo)*

» SCOTT GALLAGHER:
It's nice to see a clip-point hunter in the mix, here in an 80CrV2 high-carbon steel blade with a black Cerakote finish and a Koa handle set on a full tang. *(BladeGallery.com photo)*

« JAMIE HARRINGTON:
The CPM S35VN hunter/field knife is easy to grip in its silver needlewood handle with checkered African blackwood inlays. *(Rod Hoare photo)*

« DAVID JESSIE: Could it be that the CPM S30V "Tater" is named for its antique Westinghouse Micarta handle? *(SharpByCoop photo)*

» DE WET VAN ZYL: A hand-forged damascus san mai hunter includes an O1 tool steel core, brass guard and stabilized Kiaat wood handle. *(BladeGallery.com photo)*

« SHAWN MCINTYRE: The maker hunted some Hawaiian mango for the handle of a flat-ground 52100 fixed-blade hunting knife. *(Rod Hoare photo)*

» BRENT SANDOW: A mirror-polished 154CM drop-point hunter is ready to hit the woods in a black Micarta handle and red fiber spacers. *(SharpByCoop photo)*

» GARY RODEWALD: The "Executive" damascus hunter hits the boardroom in an ancient walrus ivory handle. *(BladeGallery.com photo)*

RYAN SIMON: With "Twisted Ws" damascus blade and Tasmanian curly blackwood handle, the hunter had me at "hello." *(Rod Hoare photo)*

JIM POLING: A clean 4.75-inch 1075 hunter is equipped with a stainless finger guard and a Brazilian rosewood handle. *(SharpByCoop photo)*

JESS HOFFMAN: The small Cork hunting knife, here in a flat-ground CPM 154 blade, has a sweeping Koa wood grip for a secure grasp while cutting. *(Jocelyn Frasier Photography)*

» CRAIG BROSMAN: From the drop-point RWL-34 blade with tapered tang to the European red stag handle, this one oozes with tradition. *(SharpByCoop photo)*

JON MOORE: The dapper hunting knife dons a bold twist-damascus blade, a pink giraffe bone handle, an Osage spacer and brass trim.

CHRIS JONES: The "Vizsla EDC" is decked out in a flat-ground Nitro V blade, and a Trustone, copper resin and Turkish walnut handle. *(Jocelyn Frasier Photography)*

ROBERT WAYMAN: A spectacular feather damascus hunter features an amboyna burl handle, and G-10, bog oak and mammoth molar spacers. *(SharpByCoop photo)*

» PETER COCKS:
The hunter is well-equipped with a mallee burl handle, G-10 liners, stainless pins and a "Starry Night" mosaic damascus blade.
(Rod Hoare photo)

RUDY DEAN:
A-hunting we will go with this 330-layer damascus beauty in antiqued brass and African blackwood. *(SharpByCoop photo)*

DAVID KELLEY:
The "Woods Walker Hunter" steps out in CPM 154 steel, bronze guard and spalted maple handle.
(Mitchell D. Cohen Photography)

MICHAEL HOBBS:
The "Lynx" leaps off the page in a 12-layer twist-damascus blade, integral bolster and stag handle.
(SharpByCoop photo)

» **DAVID HALL:**
The "Cutler Caper" is ready for work in damascus and stag.
(Mitchell D. Cohen Photography)

» **STEPHAN FOWLER:**
A gentleman's hunter boasts a ladder-pattern damascus blade, mosaic damascus guard and curly Koa handle.
(SharpByCoop photo)

» **JERRY MCJILTON:**
The "Peregrine" hunter is put together in CPM 154 steel and ironwood.
(Mitchell D. Cohen Photography)

» **JOHN CHAPMAN:**
The material makeup of a 4.5-inch drop-point hunter is AEB-L steel, nickel silver and mammoth tooth.
(SharpByCoop photo)

JACOB GAETZ: A classic drop-point hunter is handled in stabilized maple burl, bladed in 52100 steel and bolstered by feather damascus. *(Jocelyn Frasier Photography)*

BRENT DIGNAM: A hunter enters the fray in a Robert Corey Scott san mai damascus blade with 1084 core, curly maple handle and mammoth molar spacer. *(SharpByCoop photo)*

JOHN SCHULTZ: A hot little hunter showcases twist damascus, ironwood and a file-worked spacer. *(Mitchell D. Cohen Photography)*

ARNO BERNARD: Stabilized woolly mammoth molar handle scales are set on the full tang of a Bohler N690 stainless drop-point hunter. *(BladeGallery.com photo)*

ANDREW BLOMFIELD: A flat-ground 80CrV hunter is handled in ironwood creatively carved by Keanan Long. *(SharpByCoop photo)*

SANDRO BOECK: The mosaic damascus blade of a drop-point hunter handled in buffalo horn may be too pretty to use. *(BladeGallery.com photo)*

Daggers Done Right

» **JASON COY:**
Curl your fingers 'round that buckeye burl grip and gaze at the twist-damascus blade.
(Jocelyn Frasier Photography)

» **BOB EARHART:**
Lay your bets down on a 278-layer damascus dagger in a hot gun-blued guard, spacers and pommel, and a silver wire-wrapped fluted American holly handle.
(SharpByCoop photo)

CRAIG CAMERER:
Black and gray all over, the dagger is a twist-damascus dynamo in a carbon-fiber handle and Kevlar spacer. *(Mitchell D. Cohen Photography)*

« **STUART SMITH:**
An 11.25-inch, sleek dagger is done up in a "Sideways Ws" damascus blade, textured and antiqued bronze guard and fluted desert ironwood handle.
(BladeGallery.com photo)

» EYAL LANDESMAN: The folding dagger features a hand-rubbed RWL-34 blade, a zirconium handle frame and mosaic pau shell inlays. *(SharpByCoop photo)*

CARL MICHAEL ALMQVIST: The "Thor & Freya" dagger set is accomplished via Andre Andersson damascus, reindeer antler, ironwood and creative craftsmanship. *(BladeGallery.com photo)*

« JACKSON RUMBLE: An integral damascus dagger is done right in a split guard, and wire-wrapped fluted mammoth ivory handle. *(SharpByCoop photo)*

« DEON NEL: Of N690 blade steel and black Micarta, the dagger is demure, mindful. *(Mitchell D. Cohen Photography)*

» JIM POLING: Silver-plated wire wends its way around the fluted cocobolo handle of a quillon dagger in a 1095 blade and mild steel guard. *(SharpByCoop photo)*

» JEAN-PIERRE POTVIN: A pierced dagger is delivered in D2 steel, mother-of-pearl and gold inlay. *(SharpByCoop photo)*

« JUSTIN CHENAULT: A mosaic damascus dagger engages an antique bronze guard and fluted handle with twisted nickel silver wire overlay. *(Mitchell D. Cohen Photography)*

« STUART KERR: While Matt Fusco forged the feather damascus dagger blade, the maker fluted an African blackwood handle for the piece, wrapping it in sterling silver wire and hot bluing a mild steel guard. *(SharpByCoop photo)*

» CHARLES CARPENTER: A dagger is done right in "Ladder Ws"-pattern damascus, a bronze guard, and a fluted blackwood handle wrapped in twisted bronze wire. The pommel is a windowed bronze cup overtop damascus. *(Jocelyn Frasier Photography)*

« RYAN BREUER: A quillon dagger looks dapper in W1 tool steel, faux ivory and iron wire. *(SharpByCoop photo)*

« BRAD MILLMAN: Mammoth tusk and mosaic damascus make for a gorgeous combination on a 16.75-inch dagger. *(Jocelyn Frasier Photography)*

« RYAN LEWIS: A flat-ground damascus quillon dagger is done up in fluted Tasmanian blackwood and silver wire inlay. *(SharpByCoop photo)*

« CHUCK COOK: Stabilized bone and damascus never looked so smart as on this fixed dagger. *(SharpByCoop photo)*

» PEKKA TUOMINEN: An art dagger is done up in mosaic damascus and fluted cocobolo. *(SharpByCoop photo)*

CHRIS FARRELL: "Misery" loves the company of a Joe Syverson twist damascus blade, and a TruStone Malachite handle. *(SharpByCoop photo)*

DAVID LISCH: Rich is the dagger bladed in "Star-Crossed Lovers" mosaic damascus, handled in fossilized artifact walrus and guarded in pure iron covered with melted gold. *(SharpByCoop photo)*

Swords That Slay

CHUCK IANNI: Damascus patterning pools up along the centerline of a katana blade with a cord-wrapped handle. *(Mitchell D. Cohen Photography)*

J.J. SIMON: A main-gauche (left-hand) sword is decorated to the hilt in 1075-and-15N20 damascus, a nickel silver pierced and filigreed sail, or basket, and an oosic handle. *(SharpByCoop photo)*

HEATH BESCH: To anchor the 31-inch W2 blade of the katana, the maker fashions a silk-wrapped stingray skin handle with brass Koshirae mountings. *(Jocelyn Frasier Photography)*

DENIS TYRELL: The impressive Viking sword has a 30-inch mosaic damascus blade, gold-inlaid twist-damascus guard and a sharkskin handle. *(SharpByCoop photo)*

DALE WINBURN: Designed to be used with one hand, the 5160 arming sword enlists a bronze guard and pommel, and a leather-wrapped grip. *(Mitchell D. Cohen Photography)*

SETH LOPEZ: A worthy wakizashi is sent to battle in an 80CrV2 blade, copper and wrought iron tsuba (guard), a stingray skin-wrapped maple handle and a fossilized megalodon tooth menuki (handle charm). *(SharpByCoop photo)*

KEVIN CASHEN: Modeled after a 13th-century French knight's sword in the New York Metropolitan Museum of Art, the classic rendition includes an L6 blade and fire-blued fittings. *(Mitchell D. Cohen Photography)*

» JESSE HU:
A sweeping twist-damascus katana enlists a brass guard, copper habaki (blade collar) and spacers, and a steel fuchi (hilt collar) and kashira (pommel). *(Jocelyn Frasier Photography)*

« ANDERS HOGSTROM:
The "Vaenge" short sword is styled after an original found on Gotland, a Baltic island off the Swedish coast, this version in a 19.5-inch damascus blade, antiqued bronze fittings and a wenge wood handle. *(Mitchell D. Cohen Photography)*

» BROCK WOODSON:
Like a Greek god, the canine-head pommel of the Anubis sword is an impressive creature standing guard over a 1084- and 15N20-damascus blade. *(Mitchell D. Cohen Photography)*

VINCE EVANS:
An impeccable Italian Schiavona sword showcases a multi-fullered damascus blade, blackwood hilt, engraved basket and bronze mounts. *(SharpByCoop photo)*

PETER JOHNSSON:
Inspired by a group of blades from the ancient Greek world—the Machaira, Kopis, and Harpë—the "Chronokoptis" sword embodies a 700-layer organic-pattern damascus blade, an iron and fused bronze guard and a leather-wrapped wood hilt with bronze studs. *(SharpByCoop photo)*

Pinpoint Pocketknives

It's actually easy to pinpoint what makes these pocketknives special—it's pinpoint precision, precious materials, impeccable fit and finish and classic styling. Like the most modern of flipper folders, the blades open like whispers, and the friction is left for family holiday get-togethers.

When the springs, blades, pivots, and liners are in sync and of proper working order, nothing (not even assisted-opening folders, autos or butterfly knives) is more fun to handle and manipulate. Sometimes, a stiff pull on a blade followed by smooth pivot action becomes a more personal maneuver than a thumb flick or button release. When the thumbnail slides into the blade nick, and the folder gives a click, then overcoming the spring tension is as fun as flipping a butterfly knife, and not quite as dangerous, but watch those digits.

Pinpoint pocketknives blend old-school design with modern materials, springs, detents, pivots and liners, letting the knives do the talking and the blades do the walking.

» **TORY UTT:** There's more to the straight jackknife than first appears, including a Mike Norris damascus blade, Ken Steigerwalt mosaic damascus bolsters, jigged bone handle scales and a mokume-gane shield. *(SharpByCoop photo)*

RHIDIAN GATRILL: Hand-jigged worm-groove scales make up the handle half of an AEB-L saddlehorn lockback folder. *(Jocelyn Frasier Photography)*

» ALEXANDR POROSHYN: The "Harvey" model exhibits a comely recurved M390 blade, mammoth ivory handle scales, acorn shield and titanium liners and bolsters. *(Mitchell D. Cohen Photography)*

« TANNER COUCH: The shadow-pattern rabbit skinner enlists a CPM 154 blade, paper Micarta handle and frame, and copper liners and hardware. *(SharpByCoop photo)*

« BOBBY HOUSE: Despite being a doctor's knife, it sports a Vegas Forge "Virus Damascus" blade, as well as ivory handle scales, jeweled liners and CPM 154 stainless bolsters engraved by Alice Carter. *(Jocelyn Frasier Photography)*

D.R. DAVIS:
Amber stag and CPM 154 steel make up the bulk of a three-blade stockman.
(Mitchell D. Cohen Photography)

SHAWN MCINTYRE:
The slip-joint Barlow pocketknife is built with a 52100 blade, stainless bolster and antique bone handle scales. *(Rod Hoare photo)*

AARON LAWVERE:
A "Zulu spear" slip-joint folder wears a Vegas Forge "Reptilian" damascus blade, stainless bolsters and amber-stag handle scales.
(Jocelyn Frasier Photography)

» CHARLES GEDRAITIS: The handle of the maker's automatic Swiss Army Knife is inspired by the Dr. Strange character of Marvel Comics fame and includes a belt, medallion and cape. *(SharpByCoop photo)*

DAVID TUCKER: Five CPM 154 blades, amber stag handle scales, 416 stainless bolsters and integral mill-relieved liners fit together with the precision of a Swiss watch. *(Rod Hoare photo)*

« CHARLES VESTAL: A Tony Bose-pattern "Zulu" is engineered using a CPM 154 blade, stainless integral bolsters and liners, and amber stag handle scales. *(SharpByCoop photo)*

» STANLEY BUZEK:
The gent's folder sports a Mike Tyre feather-damascus blade, mammoth ivory handle scales, and an acorn handle shield and bolsters engraved by Alice Carter. *(Jocelyn Frasier Photography)*

PHILLIP GALLIA:
Of the resurging "axe handle" ilk, the CPM 154 slip-joint folder comes in natural stag. *(SharpByCoop photo)*

DANIEL KEOWN:
One clean back-pocket slip-joint folder is outfitted in antique mammoth ivory. *(Mitchell D. Cohen Photography)*

» EVAN NICOLAIDES:
Ah, the pearl-handle pocketknife, there's nothing as sweet, and the "Stingray Sportsman" in AEB-L steel and titanium is one fine example. *(SharpByCoop photo)*

« JASON RITCHIE:
The two-blade trapper looks resplendent in stag. *(Mitchell D. Cohen Photography)*

» THEODORE FRIESENHAHN:
A fancy hobo pocketknife is done up in damascus and sambar stag. *(SharpByCoop photo)*

» RHIDIAN GATRILL: The lockback "Rhiddler" whittler is a CPM 154 steel and mammoth ivory puzzle in a pretty package. *(Jocelyn Frasier Photography)*

JIM DUNLAP: An "Improved Muskrat" emerges in CPM 154 blade steel, stainless bolsters and fossil ivory handle scales. *(Mitchell D. Cohen Photography)*

BRUCE BARNETT: Send in the five-blade sowbelly, that with flat-ground CPM 154 steel and red stag. *(SharpByCoop photo)*

« GRAYSON JENNINGS: Enter the Wharncliffe trapper in etched A2 blades and stag handle scales. *(Mitchell D. Cohen Photography)*

» DAVID TABER: The maker lets a lockback whittler loose in CPM 154 blade steel and bark elephant ivory handle scales. *(SharpByCoop photo)*

« DON HANSON III: The nice W-2 single-blade folder with nail nick deserved a Matt Cullen jigged bone handle. *(SharpByCoop photo)*

« CRAIG BREWER: Damasteel and black-lip pearl dominate a three-blade stockman with rose gold shield and pins. *(Jocelyn Frasier Photography)*

» BUBBA CROUCH: A single-blade axe handle trapper is done up in Michael Tyre feather damascus and natural stag. *(Mitchell D. Cohen Photography)*

STATE OF THE ART

Working as a craftsperson in a single medium and selling one's products takes skill, determination, creativity, desire and drive. Working in multiple mediums is more impressive yet, and fashioning photo-worthy utilitarian tools that end up in the hands of edged art lovers, collectors and discerning knife enthusiasts is ultimately admirable.

"State of the Art" chapters in this *KNIVES* book cover such skilled knifemaking areas as hand-forging damascus, mosaic damascus and san mai steel blades; carving wood grips; engraving guards; sculpting knife forms; scrimshawing ivory, faux ivory, bone and other porous materials; gold inlay; stonework; woodwork; and skilled parts making.

Builders of the blades herein are true artisans working in as many mediums as it takes to fashion knives for those who appreciate the finer things in life. Embodying quality and craftsmanship, the edged tools come from the hands of those who care enough to stand behind their work. These pieces represent not only the "State of the Art" in knives, but also the makers behind them, those who stake their reputations on their products.

Collectors are known to buy pieces from makers whom they like, those whom they admire, and whose work and work ethic impress them. They savor "Blades of a Feather," "Slack-Jaw Scrimshaw," "Tasteful Engraving," "Highly Carved Creations," "Eye-Popping Timascus," and "Immersive Mosaics."

Enthusiasts can't help but admire san mai steel, copper san mai, damascus, whirling burls, steel sculptures, monumental stonework, gilding, carving and creative handle making. *KNIVES* book readers gravitate toward such skilled craftsmanship, too, and immerse themselves in the knifemaking arena.

Immersive Mosaics

All the mosaic damascus blades and bolsters within this chapter are uniquely spectacular, patterns of pounded, forged, heated, folded, shaped, cooled, etched and finished steel, sculpted and honed to keen edges, their atomic alloys gleaming. The mosaic damascus blades are works of art from forged beginnings. Born of the fire, those with infernal beginnings build character along the way.

But they are not natural beings. Those belong to the men behind the face shields and safety goggles who hold the tongs and hammer, pounding out works, whether canister steel or preformed squares, bars, rods and powder. How the steel was worked is as important as where its destiny lies.

The immersive mosaics found homes in knives designed specifically to accept the blades for harmonic form and function. Together, the knife designs and immersive mosaics flow together for the benefit of blade lovers everywhere.

« RONNIE SMITH: The aesthetic sweet spot is dead center of the highly patterned mosaic damascus blade, here substantially handled in fossil walrus ivory with copper fittings.
(Jocelyn Frasier Photography)

« PETER COCKS: Aptly named the "Desert Moth Mosaic Utility," the highly patterned drop-point fixed blade sports a spalted sassafras burl handle.
(Rod Hoare photo)

» QUINTIN T. HARDTNER: The mosaic patterning is perfectly matched to the blade shape of the bowie handled in fossilized walrus tusk with nickel silver, sterling silver and damascus fittings. *(SharpByCoop photo)*

» ANDREW WASNAC: The maker delivers a drop-point hunter in a mosaic damascus blade and stag handle. *(Mitchell D. Cohen Photography)*

» FRANK EDWARDS: A shapely mosaic damascus folder is embellished with gold Dellana dots, engraved bolsters with 24k-gold borders and hand-carved mammoth ivory handle scales. *(BladeGallery.com photo)*

« CHAD J. JONES: An elite EDC is enlivened by "Gorgan Flower" damascus and an Atzelia burl handle separated by "Zebra" carbon-fiber bolsters. *(Jocelyn Frasier Photography)*

» ANTHONY KITTEL: The winning combination of a coffin-handle bowie is mosaic damascus, brass and dyed giraffe bone. The frame is Micarta. *(Rod Hoare photo)*

» LONNIE JENSEN: The maker and Steve Schwarzer collaborated on the mosaic damascus blade, adding a wrought iron guard, a deer antler handle that's carved by Tyler Poor, and a Leigh Dunham leather sheath. *(SharpByCoop photo)*

GABE FLETCHER: The damascus patterning is dazzling on a 9.75-inch chef's knife with integral bolster and stabilized curly Koa handle. *(BladeGallery.com photo)*

MATTHEW DONALDSON: The immersive mosaic damascus Nakiri possesses a stabilized maple burl handle and bronze spacer. *(Rod Hoare photo)*

SCOTT GALLAGHER: Fossil mammoth ivory, mosaic damascus and 24k-gold inlay will make the mouth water. *(Jocelyn Frasier Photography)*

JACCO VAN DE BRUINHORST: The keyhole knife handled in desert ironwood flies its "American Flag Cluster" mosaic damascus blade with pride. *(SharpByCoop photo)*

TOMMY GANN: Not just any clip-point hunter gets a mosaic damascus blade like this, but perhaps one with a polished stainless guard and ancient walrus ivory handle. *(BladeGallery.com photo)*

MARK BARRETT: "Explosion" mosaic damascus leaves shrapnel across the blade of a Gyuto chef's knife in a Tasmanian blackwood handle and ebony spacer. It comes with a matching blackwood sheath. *(Rod Hoare photo)*

» TUCKER ABBOTT: A bold bowie ventures out in a Dillon Kology mosaic damascus blade, stainless guard and Honduran rosewood burl handle. *(Jocelyn Frasier Photography)*

« MORENO FELTRESI: It's cassia wood, mosaic damascus and the eye of a sculptor. *(SharpByCoop photo)*

« CARL MICHAEL ALMQVIST: The "Black Dragon" Swedish utility knife enters the arena in a Roger Bergh mosaic damascus blade, buffalo horn guard and pommel and a stabilized birch and bog oak handle. *(BladeGallery.com photo)*

« SAM RODDY: Classy and smooth, the lines of the 10-inch bowie are accomplished in 1084 and 15N20 mosaic damascus, nickel silver, brass and desert ironwood. *(Jocelyn Frasier Photography)*

» BRENDON GARVIN:
The sub-hilt fighter showcases a Robert Eggerling mosaic damascus blade and pommel cap, copper guard and blue and red stabilized box elder burl handle. *(SharpByCoop photo)*

« SANDRO BOECK:
A Sendero hunter is sent to market in a mosaic damascus blade, blackened steel guard and dyed giraffe bone handle. *(BladeGallery.com photo)*

» ZANE DVORAK:
The maker put his fingerprints all over the integral hunter, here in an African blackwood handle and black-edge mosaic damascus blade. *(Jocelyn Frasier Photography)*

^ RYAN SIMON:
Mosaic damascus and mammoth ivory make up the bulk of the magnificent flat-ground recurved bowie. *(Rod Hoare photo)*

» DAN TOMPKINS: Whether one sees Knights of the Templar crosses or flying albatrosses in the mosaic damascus blade of an Unagisaki (eel filleting knife) is up to the eye of the beholder, the person who grips the lace she oak handle. *(SharpByCoop photo)*

« MATTHEW PARKINSON: The pictorial mosaic damascus blade of the chef's knife shows the sun or moon setting over an ocean of patterning. *(SharpByCoop photo)*

» LEE PARSONS: If you get lost in the "Dark Matter" mosaic damascus, pull yourself out via the stag handle of the 10-inch bowie, here with copper and nickel silver spacers. *(Jocelyn Frasier Photography)*

« JARRETT CIESLAK: Rare is the bowie in a multi-bar twisted mosaic damascus blade, damascus guard and curly maple handle. (Mitchell D. Cohen Photography)

» **DAVID LISCH:** The maker forged a "Band of Brothers" mosaic damascus blade for a "C Lock" integral hunter in an ancient ivory handle. *(SharpByCoop photo)*

« **DILLON KOLOGY:** Patterned movement within an integral chef's knife is courtesy of an 8-inch mosaic damascus blade and amboyna burl handle. *(Jocelyn Frasier Photography)*

» **TANNER COUCH:** Water lilies float along the Bill Poor "Gorgon Flower" damascus blade of an axe handle trapper in ivory handle scales, and a shadow shield. *(SharpByCoop photo)*

« **JACOB GAETZ:** The fighter features a full 9 inches of mosaic damascus blade, a casehardened guard and pommel nut, and a Siamese rosewood handle. *(Joçelyn Frasier Photography)*

» STEVEN KOSTER: A fluid folding dagger is destined for the halls of greatness in a mosaic damascus blade, bolsters and clip, gold-lip mother-of-pearl handle scales, and a pearl thumb stud. *(SharpByCoop photo)*

« JOSEPH BANDEKO: The double keyhole fighter is ready to lash out with a mosaic damascus blade, curly rosewood handle and bronze guard and pommel. *(SharpByCoop photo)*

⌃ RICARDO VILAR: The fighter is outfitted with an eagle claw-style mosaic damascus blade, an engraved and gold-inlaid pommel, mammoth ivory handle scales and a free-floating gemstone in the end cap to boot. *(Jocelyn Frasier Photography)*

» JESSE HU:
A tightly patterned mosaic damascus chef's knife is the beneficiary of an amboyna burl handle with brass and bronze spacers. *(Jocelyn Frasier Photography)*

DAVID BRENIERE:
Mosaic damascus and Koa wood are combined to create a bodacious bowie. *(SharpByCoop photo)*

« JUSTIN CHENAULT:
What better bowie patterning than a "Stars and Stripes Explosion" mosaic damascus blade and a curly Koa handle? *(Mitchell D. Cohen Photography)*

» BRENT STUBBLEFIELD: A ribbon and rifle stock imagery run through the mosaic damascus blade of a 12-inch chef's knife with desert ironwood handle. *(SharpByCoop photo)*

ANDREW BLOMFIELD: The Australian knifemaker forged a stunning multi-bar mosaic damascus blade for the sub-hilt bowie that includes a spalted maple handle. *(BladeGallery.com photo)*

JORDAN BUCKLEY: The mosaic damascus blade alone is mouthwatering, let alone the meals this African blackwood-handle chef's knife is likely to prepare. *(SharpByCoop photo)*

Handled with Care

» **CHRIS RICHARDSON:** Using the champleve enameling technique of carving cells into metal and filling them in, the maker fashioned a Magnacut pill folder with a copper handle and titanium liners. He even fashioned matching cufflinks. *(SharpByCoop photo)*

» **DAVID BRODZIAK:** The chef's special this day was a Magnacut CPM blade, brass and stainless spacers, and a handle composed of coffee beans in gold resin. *(Rod Hoare photo)*

JOSE SANTIAGO-CUMMINGS: Half hunter, half masterpiece, the fixed blade features a Baker Forge "Firestorm" damascus blade, tri-metal Mokume-gane and brass bolster, and a handle of copper, black ash, buffalo horn, composite stone, maple burl and ironwood. *(Jocelyn Frasier Photography)*

» GREGER FORSELIUS: A multi-bar damascus Swedish hunting knife sports warthog tusk bolsters, and a dyed birch and cross-cut mammoth ivory handle. *(BladeGallery.com photo)*

« GAVIN HAWK: A deadlock out-the-front auto features a 20CV blade, aluminum frame and titanium handle inlays gorgeously engraved by Wilfred Valtakis II of Chipped Metal. *(SharpByCoop photo)*

» BILL KOENIG: The "Arius Osseus" Damasteel flipper folder showcases a zirconium handle grooved in a concentric ring pattern that plays out across the partitioned Koa wood grip. *(Mitchell D. Cohen Photography)*

GEOFFREY BAZE: The handsome hunter sports a low-layer damascus blade, and a pinstripe ash and blue "Fuzzy Navel Resin" handle (both materials from Flying Shark Knives), as well as a blue glow spacer in the middle. *(Jocelyn Frasier Photography)*

» CHRIS TAYLOR: The "Benton County Boot" knife sports a "Bjorkman's Twist" Damasteel blade and a hybrid maple burl and resin handle. *(Mitchell D. Cohen Photography)*

« SANDRO BOECK: Bone inlays enliven the vintage Micarta handle scales of a stainless damascus front flipper folder. *(BladeGallery.com photo)*

« MICHAEL WEST: The continuous slope of the ebony and Argentium silver handle is a nice extension of the twist Damasteel blade. This one comes with a matching fitted sheath. *(SharpByCoop photo)*

^ ANDREAS KALANI: The high-carbon steel fixed blade is the beneficiary of a carved bone handle finished with a carved and inlaid skull cap, enhancing the knife's visual appeal.

MORENO FELTRESI: The mosaic damascus fixed blades showcase composite handles consisting of cork, walnut shell powder, epoxy, clay and pumice. *(SharpByCoop photo)*

ADAM FROMHOLTZ: The 15N20 high-carbon steel steampunk slip-joint folder features nickel silver and mokume-gane bolsters, and an ebony and brass handle with parts from guitar strings and machinery. *(Rod Hoare photo)*

DAVID KELLEY: The handle of a small hunter combines natural canvas Micarta and "sunset orange" jigged bone, along with orange liners. *(Mitchell D. Cohen Photography)*

MASON BRANDA: The 4-inch Magnacut hunter boasts a handle combination of C-Tek, ironwood, carbon fiber and Micarta. *(Jocelyn Frasier Photography)*

» **MICHAEL WALKER:** An enlivened titanium handle leaps off the page, and the Vegas Forge stainless damascus blade of a "Slyder Lock" folder is no slouch, either.

(SharpByCoop photo)

« **DANIEL GUTIERREZ:** With steel by Baker Forge and Tool, the harpoon-style fixed blade features a segmented handle of hornbeam wood, carbon fiber, moose antler, woolly mammoth ivory and G-10.

(Jocelyn Frasier Photography)

JURGEN STEINAU: A mosaic of pearl is prettily planted on the handle of a credit card auto folder.

(Mitchell D. Cohen Photography)

JOT SINGH KHALSA: The fossilized coral handle of an auto folder is as mesmerizing as the Robert Eggerling damascus blade, pau shell accents and carved stainless bolsters.

» JOE MANGIAFICO: The "Brook Trout Big Canoe" favors a Rose Damasteel blade, superconductor bolsters, and a combination G-10, brass and superconductor handle. *(SharpByCoop photo)*

« NICK MARSHALL: White mother-of-pearl inlays span the length of the NTPT (North Thin Ply Technology) and white gold handle of the "Wren" folder with RWL-34 blade. *(Mitchell D. Cohen Photography)*

» CHRIS JONES: Koa wood and resin make up the handle half of an 8.25-inch chef's knife outfitted with ladder-pattern damascus. (*Jocelyn Frasier Photography)*

MANUELE MESSORI: The remarkable folder features zirconium, meteorite and mother-of-pearl inlays, including in the "Odin Heim" Damasteel blade. *(SharpByCoop photo)*

» EDWARD RATANUN: Dynamic Tiffany blue G-10 laminate handle scales pop off a LinerLock folder in a "Daupner" Damasteel blade and magnetic Carboti bolsters. *(Mitchell D. Cohen Photography)*

LONNIE JENSEN: Koa wood and acrylic are combined for the grip of a damascus folding straight razor that's anything but straight. *(SharpByCoop photo)*

» ERIC TUCH: A twist damascus Steelhead jackknife features mother-of-pearl inlaid into vintage blue fiberglass Micarta handle scales. *(Mitchell D. Cohen Photography)*

NATE "TUNA" GRANT: A warship and "U.S. Army" in titanium decorates the box elder burl handle of a flat-ground damascus bowie. *(Jocelyn Frasier Photography)*

» KEVIN CASEY: Pristine pearl handle inlays pop off the black handles of these sweet little san mai fixed blades. *(SharpByCoop photo)*

« EYAL LANDESMAN: For the titanium handle of a "Sravner" Damasteel folder, the maker creates a mosaic of black-lip-pearl inlays. *(Mitchell D. Cohen Photography)*

DARRIEL CASTON: The M390 folder features laser-etched titanium handle scales in a fresh and fabulous motif. *(SharpByCoop photo)*

« GUS CECCHINI: Cha-ching, Cecchini! This one's an "Enigma"—featuring a CPM 4V core san mai blade, mother-of-pearl inlays inside brass pockets, and a four-alloy titanium clip. It's a screwless and toolless takedown model to boot. *(Mitchell D. Cohen Photography)*

» JORDAN DANZ:
The "Switchback" AEB-L hunter switches between bog oak, Koa and resin handle materials. *(SharpByCoop photo)*

« STUART SMITH:
Why, yes, that is a mammoth molar in the middle of the gold-leaf carbon-fiber handle of a damascus bowie. *(BladeGallery.com photo)*

JOHN DOYLE:
Carved mother-of-pearl leaf inlays embellish the blackwood handle of a high-carbon-damascus folder featuring ice-blue titanium accents and hardware. *(Mitchell D. Cohen Photography)*

» MARDI MESHEJIAN:
The Japanese-inspired fixed-blade art knife includes a Buchanan tartan-clad bog oak handle in a plaid design with a matching sheath. The tartan was acquired at the infamous Islay Woollen Mill on the Isle of Islay off the coast of Scotland. *(SharpByCoop photo)*

Blades of a Feather

It took human beings over a hundred million years, many broken bones and quite a few deaths to learn how to fly. One could surmise, I suppose, that mankind has been obsessed with birds, their feathers, tails, beaks and flight patterns since the first archaeopteryx took wing sometime between the middle and late parts of the Jurassic period. Or maybe their attentions were turned more toward dinosaurs of the period.

Regardless, as far as natural forms, one could do worse than birds, wings and feathers. Perfect examples of form following function, intricately woven parts to a whole make dancing and soaring in the sky possible.

Feather damascus stopped being a trend years ago because bladesmiths never stopped forging it, and knifemakers have never stopped using steel that's patterned with what looks like vanes of feathers running lengthwise down the centers of blades and barbs splaying out toward the spines and edges. It's a match made in heaven, blades of a feather, and now mankind has a new obsession.

« NICHOLAS ORR: Feather mosaic damascus splays out from the coffin-style African blackwood handle of an 8.5-inch bowie.
(Jocelyn Frasier Photography)

« ANDREA LISCH: Feather damascus and black walnut is all it took to make a tasty chef's knife.
(SharpByCoop photo)

» ANDREW WASNAC: The "Feather Fighter" is no featherweight, here donning a feather-damascus blade and fossil walrus ivory grip. *(Mitchell D. Cohen Photography)*

JOHN HORRIGAN: The "End of Trail Bowie" parades an "interrupted feather" damascus blade, mammoth ivory handle scales, and stainless bolsters engraved with the iconic End of the Trail symbol on one side and a buffalo on the other. *(Jocelyn Frasier Photography)*

PETER BALD: A lockback folder is decked out in a feather damascus blade, red mallee wood handle, and a nickel silver frame and bolsters. *(Rod Hoare photo)*

ANDREW BLOMFIELD: A high-class bowie is born from forged feather damascus, blackened mild steel and exhibition-grade curly Koa. *(BladeGallery.com photo)*

» ROBERT WAYMAN: A wild feather damascus bowie benefits from damascus fittings and a Siam curly rosewood handle with black G-10 and nickel silver spacers.
(SharpByCoop photo)

« JEROEN KNIPPENBERG: It's as if the calamus or shaft of the feather damascus blade extends down the length of the desert ironwood handle on an integral chef's knife.
(Jocelyn Frasier Photography)

» TREVOR MORGAN JR. A perfect example of the feather pattern splaying out toward the edge and spine, the chef's knife sports an integral bolster and curly Koa handle.
(SharpByCoop photo)

« BILL KENNEDY JR.: A saddlehorn folding pocketknife is one thing, but a model in Michael Tyre feather damascus and stabilized musk ox horn is quite another.
(Mitchell D. Cohen Photography)

» TREVOR MORGAN JR.
A perfect example of the feather pattern splaying out toward the edge and spine, the chef's knife sports an integral bolster and curly Koa handle. *(SharpByCoop photo)*

CHAD J. JONES:
Sweet EDC styling includes feather damascus, "Zebra" carbon fiber and curly Koa wood. *(Jocelyn Frasier Photography)*

» ANDRE THORBURN and ANDRE VAN HEERDEN (A2):
If the feather-damascus blade of the tanto flipper folder doesn't trip your trigger, certainly the 3Cr12 stainless handle frame engraved by Ilza du Plessis will do the trick. *(BladeGallery.com photo)*

« BUBBA CROUCH:
Two Michael Tyre feather damascus blades are better than one, here on a saddlehorn trapper with natural stag handle scales and vine file work. *(Mitchell D. Cohen Photography)*

» TANNER MCFALL-HARTIGAN: The Bill Poor feather damascus blade is a beauty, surrounding itself with other good-looking company, like nickel silver, musk ox horn and Kingman turquoise. *(SharpByCoop photo)*

« BRAD MILLMAN: In a first for this KNIVES editor, the bowie boasts a "grouse feather"-pattern damascus blade and curly Tasmanian blackwood handle. *(Jocelyn Frasier Photography)*

« KEVIN CASEY: Feathers in the maker's cap include models with mother-of-pearl handles and sculpted silver guards. *(SharpByCoop photo)*

GABE FLETCHER: Between the bog oak handle and feather damascus blade, this chef's knife is so hot, it boils over. *(Jocelyn Frasier Photography)*

KELLY VERMEER-VELLA: The jury is in on "The Verdict" fighter, and the feather-damascus model is free to move about the country. *(SharpByCoop photo)*

BEN PITTMAN: In between the feather damascus blade and the D-guard of the bowie lies a walrus tusk handle. *(Jocelyn Frasier Photography)*

Monumental Stonework

The definition of sustainability—building a knife from steel and stone, from the elements of the earth as a tool for a human, is about as sustainable as it gets. Knives increase self-sufficiency by equipping their owners with versatile tools that can be used to acquire food, shelter and clothing.

When embellishing man's oldest tool with stone inlays and grips, natural beauty enhances the utilitarian aspect of the blades and increases the enjoyment of ownership and use. The stones are cold to the touch, smooth and hard, and the patterns within are mesmerizing. The playfulness of palpability and worldly wonder works its magic on collectors who are drawn to lapidary work and age-old elements of the earth.

Monumental stonework contained in the small package of a knife is a winsome juxtaposition and one worth spending some time with and admiring. The stonework herein is from the skilled hands of master craftsmen and craftswomen, those who understand the inherent beauty of nature and bring it into a handmade form.

JEREMY WHEATON: The extraordinary "Leon" CPM 154 lockback folder looks resplendent in a stainless handle with crazy lace agate inlays. *(Rod Hoare photo)*

KYLE ROYER: Splendor within the grasp of a "Serenity" dagger includes a charoite stone handle, gun blued fittings, 24k-gold inlay and a mosaic damascus blade. *(Jocelyn Frasier Photography)*

KELLY FRASIER: A dynamic fighter parades a flat-ground GoMai blade, damascus guard and sculpted 46-million-year-old Turritella agate handle. *(Jocelyn Frasier Photography)*

» STEVEN RAMOS: The "Quill" writes its own story in a CPM 154 blade, a thulite gemstone handle, and Alice Carter gold inlay and engraving. *(SharpByCoop photo)*

« SCOTT GALLAGHER: Alice Carter gold inlay and engraving envelops the lapis lazuli handle inlays of a mosaic damascus back-lock folder. *(BladeGallery.com photo)*

« JOSE SANTIAGO-CUMMINGS: The high-end chef's knife parades a Baker Forge & Steel "Tiger Mai" blade, a composite lapis lazuli handle, buffalo horn spacer with fine silver dots, cabochons, and black ash wood, among other amenities. *(Jocelyn Frasier Photography)*

BERTIE RIETVELD: Meet "Pegasus," the "Dragonskin" damascus masterpiece boasting one titanium frame, a dozen lapis lazuli handle inlays and a single stanhope lens. *(SharpByCoop photo)*

DWAYNE DUSHANE: Marvel at the green marble handle of the damascus gent's knife in engraved titanium bolsters. *(SharpByCoop photo)*

PATRICK ANTUZZI: To go with the gorgeous flint-knapped gold obsidian blade, the maker carved a Portoro marble handle. *(SharpByCoop photo)*

JOHN HORRIGAN: Of sole authorship, the maker's lockback folder features a "snowflake jade" handle, and 24k-gold inlay and engraving. *(Mitchell D. Cohen Photography)*

JEAN-LOUIS REGEL: The "Daisy Folder" is aptly named for the golden flowers dotting the bolsters of an RWL-34 folding knife with black granite handle inlays. *(Jocelyn Frasier Photography)*

Tasteful Engraving

« HERUCUS BLOMERUS: The maker enjoys giving engravers like Henk Viljoen plenty of room on his Damasteel flipper folders to work their magic. *(SharpByCoop photo)*

« HENNIE DU PLESSIS: The LinerLock front flipper folder showcases a Chad Nichols damascus blade, and Camo Carbon and engraved titanium handle scales, the latter in a koi fish motif over titanium liners. *(BladeGallery.com photo)*

« ANDREAS KALANI: The tanto showcases a high-carbon steel blade featuring deep engravings of a Ronin warrior and dragon, a spalted maple handle, damascus bolsters, carbon-fiber liners and nickel silver pins.

LEE WILLIAMS:
The "Crux" LinerLock folder with 4-inch recurved blade showcases titanium bolsters engraved by Wilfred Valtakis II. *(SharpByCoop photo)*

MANUEL MESSORI:
To complement the cold, steely glare of the Damasteel "Bifrost" blade, the maker enlisted Turrino Mauro to engrave a golden-eyed, frosty character with a pitchfork and icy demeanor! *(SharpByCoop photo)*

JOHNNY STOUT:
In New Braunfels, Texas, you fashion hollow-ground damascus folders with mammoth ivory handle scales and stainless bolsters engraved by Dale Bass. *(Jocelyn Frasier Photography)*

KELLY VERMEER-VELLA:
Considering the gold quartz handle inlays and gold "Dellana Dots" along the damascus blade, the maker enlisted the services of Alice Carter to engrave a gold rush scene complete with gold inlays. *(SharpByCoop photo)*

« JEFF HAWKINS: Troy Flaharty engraving envelops a CPM 154 lockback folder with a 416 stainless frame and bullet shield. *(Mitchell D. Cohen Photography)*

» NEELS ROOS: The "Storm Rider" is immortalized on the titanium bolsters of a front flipper folder in a hand-ground Zladinox stainless damascus blade and copper flake carbon-fiber handle. *(BladeGallery.com photo)*

» ANDREW MEERS: Silver engravings of a frog (one side of the handle) and rose (other side) accent the steel handle frame of a hollow-ground damascus folder. *(SharpByCoop photo)*

» BRIAN MILINSKI: A hollow-ground feather damascus folder is engraved by Troy Breeding and given sambar stag handle scales. *(Jocelyn Frasier Photography)*

» MAL HANNAN: The sgian dubh slides into action via a 440C blade, fiddleback redgum burl handle and brass bolsters engraved by Phil Vinnicombe. *(Rod Hoare photo)*

NATE "TUNA" GRANT: Colorful Tyler Poor laser engraving on titanium highlights the 5-inch damascus hunter in an ironwood grip. *(SharpByCoop photo)*

» DIRK LOOTS: The gold-inlaid and engraved bronze guard of an extended tang folder is as exquisite as the Bertie Rietveld damascus blade and mammoth ivory handle scales. *(SharpByCoop photo)*

« ELIOT MALDONADO: A keyhole folder showcases a 3-inch Bill Poor feather damascus blade, stainless bolsters engraved by Dale Bass and Remington jigged bone handle scales. *(Jocelyn Frasier Photography)* *(SharpByCoop photo)*

» JOHN HORRIGAN: A skeleton crew populates the bolsters of a damascus lockback folder with "silver forest agate" handle inlays and 24k-gold and ruby embellishments. *(Mitchell D. Cohen Photography)*

« BRIAN NADEAU: The Damasteel "Arch Nemesis" folder features a titanium frame gorgeously engraved by Vitalij Quaranta. *(SharpByCoop photo)*

» STEVE HOEL: Enlivened via bolster engraving by Lynton McKenzie, the jumbo Coke bottle front-lock folder rocks a 154CM blade and Rocky Mountain Bighorn handle scales. *(SharpByCoop photo)*

« PHIL DUNN: Tasteful bolster engraving highlights the gunstock slip-joint folder in a CPM 154 blade and hand-jigged paper Micarta handle scales. *(Jocelyn Frasier Photography)*

» JIM SORNBERGER: All work is by the maker, including the engraved silver and gold sheath, and gold guard and frame, on a Michael Price-style dagger in ATS-34 steel and celluloid tortoise shell handle inlays. *(SharpByCoop photo)*

« ANDRE THORBURN and ANDRE VAN HEERDEN (A2): The makers finish one out in a GoMai damascus blade with copper shim and carbon steel core, and a 3Cr12 handle frame gorgeously engraved by Panja Pojiew. *(BladeGallery.com photo)*

» MARIANNE KELLEY: Done up in Art Deco engraving by the maker, the pearl-handle hottie has a 1095-and-nickel-silver twisted basketweave-pattern blade and titanium liners. *(Jocelyn Frasier Photography)*

DWAYNE DUSHANE: Damascus, titanium and pearl never looked so good as this gorgeously engraved girl. *(SharpByCoop photo)*

» DON SYLVEST: Stainless bolsters engraved and gold-inlaid by Dale Bass are the centerpiece of a Natchez fighter in CPM 154 steel and ironwood handle scales. *(Jocelyn Frasier Photography)*

« EYAL LANDESMAN: Gold inlay and engraving by Molten Decorum surround the charoite handle inlays of a fine flipper folder with a ghost-etched Chad Nichols "Boomerang" damascus blade, including a CTS-XHP core. *(SharpByCoop photo)*

» BOB MERZ: Bolster engraving by Wes Griffin embellishes a pristine lockback folder in mother-of-pearl and CPM 154 steel. *(Jocelyn Frasier Photography)*

« TED MOORE: The blue Larry Donnely damascus blade contrasts nicely with the stainless handle frame engraved by Madeline Crumling and the black pen shell inlay. *(SharpByCoop photo)*

» JERRY MCCLURE:
A touch of classic scroll engraving is just enough on the damascus hunter in a crackled mammoth ivory handle.
(SharpByCoop photo)

« JERRY FISK:
Few saddle horn folders boast damascus blades, engraved bolsters and wood handles from one of the last trees George Washington planted. Perhaps more should.
(Jocelyn Frasier Photography)

« STEVEN RAMOS:
"Gemini" makes its presence known via a recurved CPM 154 blade, stainless guard that's engraved and gold inlaid by Alice Carter, and a lapis lazuli handle. *(SharpByCoop photo)*

JAKOB and SIMON NYLUND: Wow, when Chantal Schaschl started engraving the two-blade damascus lockback folder, she didn't stop. *(SharpByCoop photo)*

STANLEY BUZEK: The grip of the Damasteel trapper is a mesmerizing array of engraved, partitioned and inlaid stainless steel from the hands and mind of Alice Carter. *(SharpByCoop photo)*

BOBBY HOUSE: The fruit sampler showcases a Vegas Forge "Virus" damascus blade, stainless fittings engraved by Alice Carter, ivory handle scales, and jeweled, relieved and soda-blasted liners. *(SharpByCoop photo)*

Clad in San Mai Steel

Sometimes you don't know you need something until it's invented. So, thinking of it that way, maybe it's not so much of a need as a "want." We didn't know we "needed" email or texting until they became the primary ways of communication for a couple of the younger generations. No one knew they needed avocados and guacamole until the United States started importing the green fruits from Mexico. No one knew they needed airbags, cruise control, autosteer or heated seats until engineers created them.

It's unlikely that knife collectors, users and enthusiasts were becoming dissatisfied with mono-steel blades until makers and manufacturers began offering damascus, mosaic damascus and san mai steel blades. Now we need, or at the very least want, them … in a bad way. Once etched and finished, the layering and forging of multiple steel alloys make blades so much more visually attractive.

Some say practicing the traditional Japanese method of forging soft outer layers of steel together with a hard steel core makes a blade hold an edge longer and gives it toughness or shock absorbance simultaneously. Others might argue that anytime there are welds or layers of steel welded together, there's more chance for inclusions or breaking.

Whatever side of the san mai steel argument a person lands on, there's one thing for certain: the practice and resulting blades have become a hot market segment, one we didn't know we needed until just after we discovered how badly we wanted it.

« BRENT DIGNAM: The feather-core Go Mai blade by Charlie Bridges nearly steals the show on a 7-inch chef's knife with Richlite Micarta guard and spalted tamarind handle. *(SharpByCoop photo)*

» BRYAN MONTALVO: The "Bull Terrier" has bite through a Chad Nichols san mai blade with XHP core, and bark via its "Camo" carbon-fiber handle scales. *(Mitchell D. Cohen Photography)*

« RICHARD SOLER: A front flipper folder sports a san mai blade, and FatCarbon "Gold Dark Matter" handles scales set on titanium liners. *(BladeGallery.com photo)*

» DAN TOMPKINS: A rosewood handle fighter features a convex ground "Rust Belt" damascus san mai blade forged by the maker and Zach Tarbell. *(SharpByCoop photo)*

» DAVID LONGWORTH: I'll take two san mai EDC folders, please, one with a bolster-less wrought iron handle, and the other with mammoth ivory handle scales. Make them Rockback blade locks, if you would. *(SharpByCoop photo)*

DAVID HOEHLER: The cutting board is prepped for the Gyuto chef's knife featuring a san mai blade with VG-10 core and dyed and stabilized curly mango handle set on a full tang. *(BladeGallery.com photo)*

KELLY FRASIER: Stunning developments include a sculpted 46-million-year-old Turritella agate handle, a 68-layer damascus guard, and a 10-inch flat-ground GoMai blade. *(Jocelyn Frasier Photography)*

DE WET VAN ZYL: The stainless san mai blade with O1 carbon steel core mirrors clouds floating in the sky, here grounded by a dyed curly maple handle with mokume-gane bolster. *(BladeGallery.com photo)*

TREVOR MORGAN JR.: Take in the san mai chef's knife with White #1 core, damascus cladding, a curly Koa handle and integral bolster. *(SharpByCoop photo)*

» BRAD MILLMAN: Let's talk about an O-Tanto, particularly one in a 120-layer nickel-clad blade with an 80CrV2 core, a forged stainless and copper guard, and a Raffir Wood poplar burl handle. *(Jocelyn Frasier Photography)*

« MICHAEL ANDERSSON: So, here's a clamshell bowie in a san mai blade with damascus at its core, not to mention that mammoth ivory handle. *(BladeGallery.com photo)*

« CHARLIE LLOYD: The san mai blade may just have been struck by lightning, or forged to leave a mark, and complemented by a blued mild steel guard and stag grip. *(SharpByCoop photo)*

« CARLOS QUEIROS: The quality cutter comes to market in a Damacore "Odin's Eye" san mai blade, a FatCarbon handle, zirconium bolsters and a titanium frame. *(Mitchell D. Cohen Photography)*

DAVE SKINNER:
A Sujihiki slicer sports a hand-forged damascus san mai blade with a VG-10 core, and a stabilized Angelim Pedra (angel's heart) wood handle. *(BladeGallery.com photo)*

PATRICK HARP:
The D-guard fighter enlists a Baker Forge and Tool san mai blade, curly Koa handle, clamshell steel guard, stainless spacers and wrought iron pommel nut. *(SharpByCoop photo)*

MAXIME BELZUNCE:
Built to last, the front flipper folder incorporates a san mai blade, vapor-blasted titanium bolsters and vintage World War II Micarta handle scales. *(BladeGallery.com photo)*

» BERTIE RIETVELD: Enter the "Dragonskin" san mai damascus dagger in a titanium frame and pommel, gold inlay, and a stanhope lens. *(SharpByCoop photo)*

» JOEY DELLO RUSSO: The "Sakimaru Takobiki" showcases a double-edged 80CrV2-15N20-and-wrought-iron san mai blade, a brass bolster and desert ironwood handle. *(Jocelyn Frasier Photography)*

JORDAN BERTHELOT: The chef's knife features a ladder-pattern "BronzeMai" blade with wavy ridge line, a carbon-fiber bolster and stabilized maple burl handle. *(BladeGallery.com photo)*

Eye-Popping Timascus

» **PATRICK FAMIN:** An out-the-front auto is equipped with a san mai blade, Damasteel bolsters and an eye-popping Timascus handle. *(Mitchell D. Cohen Photography)*

» **DAN THORNBURG:** Odd bedfellows come together beautifully on a flipper folder, including Aegir pattern Damasteel, ancient walrus ivory, and raindrop Timascus. *(Jocelyn Frasier Photography)*

» **MAXIME BELZUNCE:** There's a lot to like about the front flipper, featuring an RWL-34 stainless blade, white Timascus bolsters and vintage Micarta handle scales set on titanium liners. *(BladeGallery.com photo)*

» **HERUCUS BLOMERUS:** Black Timascus handle inlays are surrounded by Henk Viljoen engraving on the zirconium frame of a flipper folder with a Takefu SG2 blade. *(SharpByCoop photo)*

» JOHN BARKER: The "Hokkaido" is constructed of CTS-XHP steel, a Timascus frame, titanium overlays and CarboQuartz inlays. *(Mitchell D. Cohen Photography)*

» KIRBY LAMBERT: The "Phoenix" rises above the rest in Vegas Forge "Reptilian" damascus, Alpha Supply Timascus and Westinghouse Ivorite paper Micarta. *(SharpByCoop photo)*

» HENNIE STEENKAMP: The Damasteel blade of a front flipper folder rides on caged ceramic ball bearings, folding into the titanium handle frame that features Timascus inlays. *(BladeGallery.com photo)*

» JIM VANDEVELD: With a "BROmascus" blade forged by the maker and Logan Gilliham, the "Transient" features a dark Timascus handle frame and zirconium accents. *(Mitchell D. Cohen Photography)*

Highly Carved Creations

» **PAUL DISTEFANO:**
While each of the mammoth ivory spacers of a mosaic damascus art dagger is carved in a "floral wreath with blooming flowers" motif, the African blackwood handle depicts an eucalyptus tree and abundant leaves that shelter fruit bats. *(SharpByCoop photo)*

JOSH NAVARRETE:
An 80CrV2 bowie boasts a carved horsehead pommel done in sambar stag. *(Mitchell D. Cohen Photography)*

CRISTIAN SILVA:
A zombie face emerges from the carved ebony handle of a small cleaver with a 3.1-inch satin-finished 1095 blade. *(BladeGallery.com photo)*

» **LONNIE JENSEN:** A carved hickory haft is always a selling point for a twist-damascus spike tomahawk. *(SharpByCoop photo)*

» **FRANK EDWARDS:** How the maker carved the white mother-of-pearl handle scales to continue the scrollwork from the damascus bolsters of the mosaic damascus folder is most impressive. *(BladeGallery.com photo)*

» **FRANCK SOUVILLE:** Crabs took shape under Alex DuBois's carving knife for the mammoth ivory handle of a damascus folder. *(SharpByCoop photo)*

Dreams of Damascus

You might not be able to make this stuff up, but if you dream it, you can create it, or at least the skilled craftsmen and women who pounded out the blades in this section can. What beautiful dreams they have, and the execution of said subconscious visions is flawless. Like a punch-drunk boxer, when gazing at the damascus, you might see stars, satellites, galaxies or planets. Some might conjure up images of animal stripes, fangs, saliva or fur, while others envision leaves, branches, tree bark or sap.

Like ink blot tests or Spirograph paper, there are no wrong ways to appreciate the shapes, forms and patterns therein. No big cat coat is the same, nor are snowflakes, fingerprints, flowers or dreamlike damascus blades.

Dreams of damascus might involve exotic warriors in stoic stances holding sharp, patterned-welded swords, or maybe bespectacled gentlemen in feathered caps, button-down coats, and wool slacks using patterned blades to peel apples. More often, the dreamlike scenes are centered on the steel itself, the mesmerizing lines and repeating patterns that put one into a state of contented slumber, free to enjoy visions of campfires, lightning bugs, moonlit skies and shooting stars.

» TOMMY GANN:
If all integral damasacus utility tantos looked like this, no one would buy anything else, here with mammoth ivory handle inlays.
(BladeGallery.com photo)

KELLY VERMEER-VELLA:
Warning, the damascus blade can cause dizziness and seizures for those who are prone to motion sickness. Hold onto the water buffalo handle and rub the gold for luck.
(SharpByCoop photo)

JON MOORE:
Forged from bearings and a timing chain, the damascus fixed blade is outfitted with a giraffe bone handle, brass trimming, and a rattlesnake skin inlaid leather sheath.

TONY DOCHERTY:
A black G-10 handle and twist-damascus blade pair nicely on a keyhole integral camp knife. *(Rod Hoare photo)*

PEARCE RICHARDSON:
The 15-inch damascus dagger blade is a doozy, combined here with a sculpted damascus guard, elk antler handle, and 18k-gold inlays and overlays.
(SharpByCoop photo)

ANDERS HOGSTROM:
Depending on how you look at the "Vulturii" art knife in Damasteel, bronze and fossil ivory, it's either a sitting parrot with head and tail feathers or a sinister bird of prey with a sharp beak. *(Mitchell D. Cohen Photography)*

STEPHANE ESPI:
The tightly patterned boot-ground Damasteel blade shimmers on a front flipper folder with a contoured titanium handle. *(BladeGallery.com photo)*

MARK SINCLAIR:
A Gyuto chef's knife is dressed in chevron-pattern damascus and a stabilized black Mulga wood handle. *(Rod Hoare photo)*

JIM PROVOST:
It took a large and in-charge bowie/fighter to properly showcase the "Grosse Rosen Damasteel" blade handled in stag horn. *(SharpByCoop photo)*

BRIAN BROWN:
Just can't get enough of that Fafnir Damasteel blade on the "Mini Warthog #18" folder in a full-titanium frame with "Dino Hide" texturing and zirconium inlays. *(Mitchell D. Cohen Photography)*

NEVILLE SHARP:
The "Scrapmascus Integral Camp Knife" is emboldened by its 1084-and-15N20 powder damascus blade and G-10 handle.
(Rod Hoare photo)

JAYDEN SIMISKY:
A furiously patterned Richter damascus blade makes a bold statement on a chef's knife with integral bolster and stabilized curly Koa handle. (*BladeGallery.com photo*)

SHAYNE CARTER:
Damascus patterning emanates from the flat-ground blade of a bowie handled in Koa wood.
(SharpByCoop photo)

RUDY DEAN:
The fighter is executed exquisitely in a 136-layer heat-colored damascus blade, nickel silver guard and spacer, and a stag handle. (*Jocelyn Frasier Photography*)

« GABE FLETCHER: An integral chef's knife has an off-the-hook damascus blade anchored by an ancient bog oak handle. *(Jocelyn Frasier Photography)*

» SAM ZIEGLER: The maker forged the damascus chef's knife blade from reclaimed tool steels, adding a bronze spacer and stabilized yellow boxwood handle. *(Rod Hoare photo)*

» DENNIS FRIEDLY: Making good use of Mike Norris and Robert Eggerling damascus, the bowie/fighter is the beneficiary of a mammoth tooth handle. *(SharpByCoop photo)*

» JEREMY MARSH: The "Black Swan" is all dolled up in Damasteel and mammoth molar. *(Mitchell D. Cohen Photography)*

VINCE EVANS:
"Cinquedea" literally means "five fingers," describing the width of the blade next to the handle, so the maker made grooves in the damascus as a visual aid on the Italian short sword, that with engraved brass and bronze guard and pommel, and ebony handle. It slays!
(SharpByCoop photo)

HENNIE STEENKAMP:
The flipper folder sports a ferocious "Fafnir"-pattern Damasteel blade, heat-colored zirconium bolsters and Timascus handle scales.
(BladeGallery.com photo)

GABE FLETCHER:
The damascus blade of a Chinese cleaver is impressively produced, as is the stabilized curly mango grip.
(BladeGallery.com photo)

MARCO LOURENCO:
The "Iridescent New York Special" showcases a 4-bar Turkish Twist damascus blade, African ebony handle, and mother-of-pearl pins.
(SharpByCoop photo)

» JOSH FISHER:
In a nice attempt to counterbalance that gorgeous 1080-and-15N20-damascus blade, the maker hand-checkered the mammoth ivory handle of a 3.5-inch hunter.
(Jocelyn Frasier Photography)

BARRY BARNARDT:
The "Fafnir"-pattern Damasteel blade is breathtaking, nicely paired with FatCarbon "Gold Dark Matter" handle scales.
(BladeGallery.com photo)

DAVID LISCH:
A pierced ring-guard bowie boasts a fantastic "Dragon Spine" damascus blade, fossilized artifact walrus ivory handle, and gold spacer. *(SharpByCoop photo)*

STANLEY BUZEK:
Gorgeously engraved by Alice Carter, the Texas trapper includes a mammoth ivory handle and Bill Poor "Gorgon Flower" damascus blade.
(Jocelyn Frasier Photography)

NICO BOSMAN: Damasteel's "Fafnir" pattern is making waves, literally, here on a featherweight flipper with antique Westinghouse Micarta handle scales and anodized crystalline titanium bolsters. *(BladeGallery.com photo)*

SETH LOPEZ: Let loose the recurved integral fighter fashioned from damascus and desert ironwood burl. *(SharpByCoop photo)*

KIRK MARBERRY: The flipper folder is dressed to the hilt from its Chad Nichols "Iguana" damascus blade to the groovy copper bolsters and green canvas Micarta scales. *(Mitchell D. Cohen Photography)*

RHIDIAN GATRILL: The safety hunter showcases a Tommy Gann damascus blade, stag handle scales, and stainless liners and bolsters. *(Jocelyn Frasier Photography)*

JORDAN BORSTELMANN: Not your average hickory-handled axe, the pattern-welded head is heavy stuff where interior lines follow outer shape. *(SharpByCoop photo)*

JUSTIN CHENAULT: A fossil walrus ivory-handle sub-hilt fighter sports nickel silver fittings and a damascus blade with patterning akin to rows of cemetery crosses. *(Mitchell D. Cohen Photography)*

NATE "TUNA" GRANT: "Dragonskin" damascus from Bertie Rietveld sets the design of a utility knife in motion, helped along by a laser-engraved titanium handle with nickel silver inlays and fiber liners. *(Jocelyn Frasier Photography)*

TORY UTT: The maker's black damascus is a nice counterpart to the Richlite handle and Ken Steigerwalt mosaic damascus bolster between them. *(SharpByCoop photo)*

» BILL MILLER:
A 14-inch bowie is the beneficiary of a 288-layer ladder-pattern damascus blade, sambar stag handle and engraving by Andrew Adams. *(Jocelyn Frasier Photography)*

» JORDAN BUCKLEY:
The wave pattern damascus blade of a Santoku chef's knife has a jet black edge that complements an antique bronze bolster and Arizona desert ironwood handle.
(BladeGallery.com photo)

« ANDREW BLOMFIELD:
The fiddleback red gum handle of the sub-hilt fighter sent shockwaves across the blade.
(SharpByCoop photo)

» BEN PITTMAN:
Stand up and salute the American flag and "Crushed Radial Ws" damascus blade of an English walnut-handle hunter. *(Jocelyn Frasier Photography)*

Sculptural Integrity

Showing integrity has never been more important than it is now in a world of misinformation, grandstanding, positioning and political finagling. Most known knifemakers don't participate or have any patience for propaganda, outsized bragging or pompous egotism. They make knives, often in shops built by their own hands with machines purchased new or secondhand, cared for, oiled, retooled and adapted.

Those folks who fashion collectible art knives ply their trades by hand as well—carving, sculpting, engraving, scrimshawing, jewel inlaying and bladesmithing. While all are creative endeavors to be admired, it's the sculptors who amaze me the most, not because their work is superior or more detailed, but rather that it makes my muscles ache thinking about the time and effort to either file or drill through steel and then polish and finish it. My arms tire after hand-sanding an old wooden chair for 10 minutes, so I can't imagine hours upon hours spent filing off steel burrs or polishing metal that these masters of the art perform daily.

Sculptural integrity is a fitting title for this chapter because to see such difficult projects through from start to finish for the sake of art takes integrity. I applaud you.

« WOLFGANG LOERCHNER: The integral 440C dagger is filed and sanded by hand, including the carved gold, black-lip-pearl and Bertie Rietveld damascus handle inlays. *(SharpByCoop photo)*

« JOT SINGH KHALSA: A natural gem-grade lapis lazuli-handled dagger showcases an 18-karat white and yellow solid gold crossguard, pommel and collars encrusted with 7 carats of fine full-cut diamonds, a sculpted stainless damascus blade bordered in 24-karat gold, and a large, faceted peridot set in gold in the pommel. The diamond settings, engraving and gold inlay on the blade are by Julie Warenski-Erickson.

JEAN-PIERRE POTVIN:
This one's sharp and a sculpture, made up of AEB-L steel and some copacetic carbon fiber. *(SharpByCoop photo)*

OLIVER GOLDSCHMIDT:
The "Terra" integral fixed blade is one piece of 52100 carbon steel and a lot of sculpting and finishing.
(Mitchell D. Cohen Photography)

RICK LALA:
The maker took Damasteel, titanium, horn and sterling silver, and arrived at this morbidly fantastic masterpiece.
(SharpByCoop photo)

BOB APPLEBY:
The maker showed his handwork on the hollow silver grip of a CPM 154 art dagger.
(SharpByCoop photo)

« ANDREAS KALANI:
"Vehrath" enters this galaxy in a deeply engraved high-carbon steel blade resembling dragon skin, and a sculpted cast bronze talon-like handle.

BERTIE RIETVELD:
The "Griffin Axe 2.0" is not just a pretty piece of heat-colored "Nebula" damascus, but rather a sculpted work of functional art in an anodized titanium handle, meteorite fittings, and a double-sided griffin head carving with stanhope lens eyes.
(SharpByCoop photo)

ED SOL:
The fully integral chef's knife is completely fashioned from acid-etched and sculpted 1095 tool steel. *(Mitchell D. Cohen Photography)*

» RYAN BREUER:
An Egyptian dagger is executed in mosaic damascus forged by the maker and friend, Jason Morrissey. It features cast bronze and a sculpted wrought iron-and-nickel pommel.
(SharpByCoop photo)

The Whirly Burls

» JAMES CROWELL: The temper line of the flat-ground W2 blade leads nicely into the highly patterned desert ironwood handle. *(Jocelyn Frasier Photography)*

» MATT PARKINSON: The stabilized maple handle of the damascus paring knife is syrupy sweet. *(SharpByCoop photo)*

» DAVID KELLEY: Spalted maple is the sticky-sweet handle material of a 1075 bowie with bronze guard and spacer. *(Mitchell D. Cohen Photography)*

GREGER FORSELIUS: A fine boning/fillet knife parades a Randy Haas damascus blade and dyed and stabilized chestnut burl handle scales set on white G 10. *(BladeGallery.com photo)*

MERT TANSU: A Tasmanian Huon pine handle proves an inspired choice for a Wootz chef's knife with mokume-gane bolster. *(Rod Hoare photo)*

JIM POLING: A flat-ground 1075 fighter is prepared in a damascus bolster and Koa wood handle with stainless domed pins. *(SharpByCoop photo)*

MICHAEL BLACK: Black ash burl gets the party started on a 9.5-inch chef's knife with a W2 blade, wispy temper line, and African blackwood bolster. *(Jocelyn Frasier Photography)*

TRE HILL: Snakewood displays its markings on a Bunka chef's knife, as does the Damasteel blade. *(BladeGallery.com photo)*

» BRENDAN ATKINSON: Red gum burl is the sticky-sweet handle material of a 15.35-inch Nitro-V stainless bowie. *(Rod Hoare photo)*

ERIK FRITZ: A hand-forged 80CrV2 chef's knife showcases a stainless bolster and double-dyed, stabilized maple burl handle scales. *(BladeGallery.com photo)*

FRANCOIS MAZIERES: York gum burl is the grip of choice for an everyday carry knife featuring a Sup-9 (5155) tool steel blade, stainless guard, and mammoth ivory and black and white G-10 spacers. *(Rod Hoare photo)*

» DAN LEWIS: An 80CrV2 coffin-handle bowie and drop-point hunter are handsomely handled in ironwood burl. *(SharpByCoop photo)*

DAVID HOEHLER:
A double-dyed and stabilized maple burl handle takes its rightful place on a fillet/boning knife, sporting a Sandvik 14C28N stainless blade.
(BladeGallery.com photo)

LEE BARKER:
The "Eastern Uro" hunter is done up in a hollow-ground "Dance Twist" Damasteel blade, stainless guard, alder burl, and Australian rosewood handle.
(Rod Hoare photo)

JASON COY:
Spalted oak makes its presence known on a 3.5-inch 80CrV2 drop-point hunter with a bronze guard. *(Jocelyn Frasier Photography)*

IAN ROGERS:
Stabilized amboyna burl and carbon fiber make up the handle half of a sleek damascus slicer. *(BladeGallery.com photo)*

JAMIE HARRINGTON:
Tasmanian blackwood kicks up a storm on a Zulu spear point in a random-pattern damascus blade and stainless shield. *(Rod Hoare photo)*

» IBIS CUTLERY: Creative cutlery creation involves 1084-and-15N20 damascus blades, buffalo horn spacers and snakewood handles. *(SharpByCoop photo)*

» DON SYLVEST: Cottonwood handle scales lie against the stainless bolsters of a CPM 154 "Trinity" LinerLock folder. *(Jocelyn Frasier Photography)*

« JARRETT CIESLAK: Mosaic damascus and curly mango are the main ingredients of a Gyuto chef's knife. *(Mitchell D. Cohen Photography)*

^ RICHARD KEMP: An Australian hunter integrates a 1084 blade, blue G-10 liners and a miniritchie wood handle. *(Rod Hoare photo)*

« BRIAN MILINSKI: Amboyna burl and Hawaiian Koa tag team the handle of a hunter with a 3.25-inch Bill Poor feather damascus blade. *(Jocelyn Frasier Photography)*

« GABRIEL MABRY: Dyed and stabilized box elder burl beautifies a bird & trout knife outfitted with an antiqued 80CrV2 blade. *(BladeGallery.com photo)*

PETER COCKS: Red Morrel burl handles the flat-ground damascus hunter just fine, thank you. *(Rod Hoare photo)*

« ANDREW SMITH: One wants to get his or her hands on that walnut haft and swing the "Twisted Ws" damascus head. *(BladeGallery.com photo)*

» ANDREW BLOMFIELD: Whether the eyes alight first on the damascus blade or stabilized spalted maple handle, there's patterning aplenty. *(SharpByCoop photo)*

BILLY PEARCE:
The clean lines of a 1075 utility fixed blade are furthered by the Bocote wood handle and red G-10 liners.
(Rod Hoare photo)

BRION TOMBERLIN:
Turkish walnut makes an appearance on the "Little River Fighter" featuring a "Ladder Ws"-pattern damascus blade.
(Jocelyn Frasier Photography)

GARY RODEWALD:
A raised-clip hunter arrives at camp in a 240-layer damascus blade and a stabilized Bocote wood handle set on a full tang.
(BladeGallery.com photo)

SASHA ROSENFELD:
A carving set is creatively crafted from 1080-and-15N20 damascus, stainless steel and amboyna burl.
(BladeGallery.com photo)

» JERRY HOSSOM: "Revenge" is sweet, here in Alabama damascus, a Micarta bolster and spalted oak handle. *(Mitchell D. Cohen Photography)*

« DERICK KEMPER: The multi-bar damascus axe is expertly handled here in purple heart and maple. *(SharpByCoop photo)*

» JOSH OSBORNE: A big ol' forged camp knife comes in a 5160 high-carbon steel blade, and a Bocote and African blackwood handle. *(BladeGallery.com photo)*

« AIDAN DE FAZIO: Orange G-10 pins set off the dyed and stabilized curly birch handle of a W2 high-carbon steel utility knife with wispy hamon (temper line). *(Rod Hoare photo)*

» GREG MANDER: The ringed Gidgee handle of a 100-layer damascus straight razor has a raw but rewarding edge. *(Rod Hoare photo)*

CHRIS FARRELL: The W2 "Mutt" fixed blades are mixed breeds of stabilized wood and acrylic-handle beasts. *(SharpByCoop photo)*

Knife Gilders

As gold increases in value, so do fine art knives tastefully embellished with golden touches here and there, whether entire knife parts, inlays or fancy engraving. Gold elevates models by some of the world's most skilled knifemakers to the status of sophisticated works of edged art. Collectors gravitate toward gold-, silver- and jewel-inlaid folders and fixed blades from the hands of master craftsmen.

The golden scrolls, locks of golden hair, fine 24-karat file work, and gold inlays, overlays and encrustations are waiting for the discerning eyes of the collector to sparkle in admiration. Function meets finery at the edge/embellishment junction where sharpened steel shares space with golden handles, bolsters and pins. Even the blades are embellished with gold when knife gilders get their hands on them, and that's the allure of precious metalwork highlighting utilitarian works of art. They truly are golden gobs of goodness.

« MICHAEL WALKER: Gold inlays grace the titanium handle of a sculpted stainless damascus "EZ Slider" dress locking folder. *(SharpByCoop photo)*

» KELLY VERMEER-VELLA: The aptly named "Spellbound" dagger showcases a "Hot Flash" pattern damascus blade, a gold-inlaid, hot-blued guard, and a mild steel handle with "Spirograph" damascus frame and Alice Carter gold inlay and engraving. *(Mitchell D. Cohen Photography)*

DAVID BRODZIAK: Gold fleck is inlaid into the banksia nut handle of a stainless damascus hunter with a VG-10 core. *(Rod Hoare photo)*

» HENNIE DU PLESSIS: The maker engraved a mermaid and gave her golden locks and scales for the titanium handle of a flipper folder with a Chad Nichols damascus blade. *(BladeGallery.com photo)*

^ JORDAN LAMOTHE: A collaboration with Jeremy Yelle and Ulysse Robert, the 9-inch damascus bowie boasts a grooved African blackwood handle, wrought iron spacer and pommel and a steel guard embellished in 24k-gold Koftgari. *(Jocelyn Frasier Photography)*

» STANLEY BUZEK: Gold vine-and-leaf inlay and engraving by Alice Carter spans the pearl handle scales and stainless bolsters of a Damasteel lockback trapper, including Dellana blade opening dots. *(SharpByCoop photo)*

« HARVEY DEAN: Gold dots and inlays populate the dog bone dagger of feather damascus and sole authorship. *(Mitchell D. Cohen Photography)*

DAVID LONGWORTH: Touches of gold along the blade, bolsters and pommel highlight the damascus rocker lock folder, featuring black-lip-mother of pearl inlays and a California opener. *(SharpByCoop photo)*

MATTHEW PARKINSON: The "Sunset" mosaic damascus blade of the "Whalerman Chef" knife features gold-plated etching to go along with the bronze bolster and toasted maple handle. *(Jocelyn Frasier Photography)*

EYAL LANDESMAN: Gold follows the shape of the mother-of-pearl handle inlays, making room for black-lip pearl, on an RWL-34 gent's folder. *(Mitchell D. Cohen Photography)*

JACCO VAN DE BRUINHORST: A pair of curvaceous twist-damascus integral fixed blades is embellished with 24k-gold vinework patterns. *(SharpByCoop photo)*

» KEVIN HARVEY: Gold scrollwork brings the hand-forged "Radiating Ws"-pattern damascus blade and hand-contoured olive burl handle together. *(BladeGallery.com photo)*

« MARIANNE KELLEY: "Baby Sister" folder is brought to life in a twisted basketweave-pattern damascus blade and a wrought iron handle with 24k-gold overlays. *(Jocelyn Frasier Photography)*

» JEAN-PIERRE POTVIN: The keyhole fixed blade is done up in heat-blued damascus, bog oak, and 14k-gold inlays along the blade spine. *(SharpByCoop photo)*

JAVIER VOGT: A guard-release auto is elaborately furnished in a forged-to-shape Doug Ponzio "Turkish Lace" damascus blade, twist damascus bolsters, 24k-gold inlays, and red deer stag handle scales. *(Mitchell D. Cohen Photography)*

DELLANA: Your daily dose of Dellana (and everyone needs a daily dose of Dellana) comes to you in a damascus blade, a sterling silver and 14k-gold guard, and an ebony handle gilded in gold and adorned with rubies. *(SharpByCoop photo)*

JOHN HORRIGAN: A tightly patterned damascus bowie blends a fossilized walrus tusk handle with twisted 18k-gold wire, and 24k-gold leaves and vines. *(Mitchell D. Cohen Photography)*

HERUCUS BLOMERUS: An exquisite flipper folder showcases a Damacore Hakkapella blade and full-scale engraving and gold inlay by Julien Marchal. *(SharpByCoop photo)*

» LUIZ GUSTAVO-GONCALVES: If Turkish damascus, 24k-gold overlays and green sapphires are your thing, then this integral piece might be for you.

(SharpByCoop photo)

JURGEN STEINAU: Imagine performing daily cutting chores using a rose gold credit card auto folder.

(Mitchell D. Cohen Photography)

» KEN STEIGERWALT: Elegant triangular gold details highlight a damascus Art Deco lockback folder with black-lip-pearl grip.

(Mitchell D. Cohen Photography)

Copper San Mai

» **BEN EUSTACE:** A Baker Forge double-damascus blade with copper makes up the business half of a K-tip European chef's knife, this in a stabilized black palm handle. *(Rod Hoare photo)*

« **DAVID MURPHY:** Not your average everyday carry knife, the winning combination includes antique Westinghouse ivory Micarta and a Baker Forge & Steel "Firestorm Ripple" blade. *(Jocelyn Frasier Photography)*

« **STANLEY BUZEK:** The maker outfits his trapper model with Adam Deville copper san mai steel, a Dichrolam carbon-fiber handle infused with real copper flakes, and Alice Carter's insanely gorgeous bolster engraving. *(SharpByCoop photo)*

» **ALEX HOSSOM:** The Yanagiba sashimi knife blends a Baker Forge "Dark Mai" copper san mai blade with a Koa handle and ebony bolsters. It comes with matching chopsticks. *(Mitchell D. Cohen Photography)*

TRE HILL:
The beautiful Bunka chef's knife showcases a nickel damascus san mai blade with copper cladding and an Aogami 2 carbon steel core, an Acrylester bolster, G-10 spacers and a dyed and stabilized curly maple handle. *(BladeGallery.com photo)*

MARK CORDINA:
The maker's Signature Series chef's knife features an OB Steel Cu-Mai blade with an Aogami Super core, a copper frame and a Ceylon ebony handle. *(Rod Hoare photo)*

JARED OESER:
The dynamic folding tanto features a copper-infused "Spirograph" san mai blade by Vegas Forge and a CamoCarbon "Space Weave" handle. *(Mitchell D. Cohen Photography)*

PAT BIGGIN:
Green hemp wood and 1084 copper san mai steel add brilliance to a utility knife with an engraved brass bolster. *(Jocelyn Frasier Photography)*

» DANE STANDEN: "Double damascus Cu Mai" is how the maker describes the prettily patterned blade of the flat-ground kitchen knife with ringed Gidgee handle and Cu Mai copper pins. *(Rod Hoare photo)*

CHRIS FARRELL: An impressive "CuMai" damascus blade is anchored by a wrought iron and copper guard, stabilized wood handle, and mosaic pins. *(SharpByCoop photo)*

» BROCK WOODSON: The colorful tanto sports a copper Cu Mai blade with an oil slick finish. *(Mitchell D. Cohen Photography)*

» ANDRE THORBURN and ANDRE VAN HEERDEN (A2): The combination of a Chad Nichols mokume-gane handle with Damasteel bolsters and a stainless Yu-Shoku mokume-gane blade clad with premium VG-10W is quite stunning. *(BladeGallery.com photo)*

« SILAS DUNNE: The chef's knife is prepared in a Baker Forge copper san mai blade and a ringed Gidgee handle. *(Rod Hoare photo)*

Slack-Jaw Scrimshaw

Scrimshaw is so pure an art form that there can never be deviation, right? It's so straightforward—ink and needles poking holes in ivory or faux ivory, delivering hues below the surface of the medium and thus permanently painting the substructure. Pictures are painted one pinprick at a time.

But knifemakers and embellishers have never been the conventional sorts, and there are laws about using ivory that's not of a certain age—you can't legally harvest or use it. So that's it, right? Not so fast. What if they scrimshawed mother-of-pearl, buffalo horn or antler? Can one paint pictures one pinprick at a time on material that's not ivory? Of course, one can! Weren't some of the first scrimshawed works on whale teeth?

Ancient ivory remains in play, and the overall results are magnificent, of course. Skilled scrimshanders ply their trade on whatever natural and synthetic materials are available, poking, etching and scratching their way to slack-jaw scrimshaw that leaves those in looking distance with mouths agape and eyes in wide wonder.

BLAKE NICHOLS: Scrimshaw artist Charles W. Connor III realistically captures a Black Lab retrieving a mallard on the walrus ivory handle of a hunter that also includes a Greg Shahan damascus blade. *(SharpByCoop photo)*

RHIDIAN GATRILL: To scrimshaw a standard-size ivory knife handle is a feat, but to do it in miniature on a 1 1/8-inch-closed Barlow is masterful. *(Jocelyn Frasier Photography)*

JEAN-PIERRE POTVIN: From where doth thou get thy stripes? But from the damascus, my friend, and the scrimshaw needle on buffalo horn. *(SharpByCoop photo)*

JIMMIE SMITH: For his single-blade stainless trapper, the maker scrimshawed a trapper on one side of the resin ivory handle, and a bear trap on the other, engraving grizzly paws on the bolsters. *(SharpByCoop photo)*

MANUELE MESSORI: The "Draupner Damasteel" folder itself is as ferocious as the hybrid tiger scrimshawed in mother-of-pearl by Luca Roccaforte. *(SharpByCoop photo)*

FACTORY TRENDS

New knife companies are putting out some incredible production knives, and when you combine those with established cutlery operations, the number of enterprises making quality blades is beyond exciting. Everyone benefits from steep competition in manufacturing man's oldest tool—the users and collectors, blue-collar workers and office exectives, sportsmen and armchair enthusiasts, those who go into harm's way and others who enjoy the weekend warrior lifestyle.

In the not-too-distant past, when knife companies offered quality steels, handle materials, and sheaths, the resulting edged tools and weapons were considered top-of-the-line models. That's not enough anymore. Knives have become complete packages with modern carry modes, locks and opening mechanisms, and high-end, often aesthetically pleasing lines, liners, bolsters, guards, pommels and frames.

Factory knives have adopted many of the same utilitarian elements as handmade blades—ceramic bearings, dimpled handles, thumb notches, studs and ramps, blade fullers, double edges, bank vault-solid locks, blade coatings, superior synthetic handles, various high-quality blade coatings and finishes, utilitarian guards and handy clips.

Often, one side of the knife is completely different from the other—perhaps there's a handle scale on the non-lock side of a folder and a plain titanium frame on the other. The handles are ergonomically engineered to be comfortable in the average hand, or made for lefties or righties, men or women, big and tall or short and petite. Safety is a concern, with not only form-fitting, snapping, locking and low- or high-carry sheaths, but also smooth handle edges, guards, non-slip grips and finger choils.

Factory trends in knives today have more to do with the design and engineering of quality, utilitarian, tough models that stay true and stand the test of time than they do with gadgets, wizardry and the latest snake oil. Precision engineering, as well as quality materials and manufacturing, are trending in today's factory knives.

SLEEK FOLDING KNIVES

A lanky breed of factory folding knives fueling consumer demand includes the Spartan Blades "Nemec" designed by Ondrej Nemec, Spyderco's "Ikuchi" model, the CRKT Stylus designed by Ken Onion, and Coast Knives LX502, which is part of the company's "Founder's Series."

BLUE-COLLAR BLADES

Perfect for the blue-collar guys and gals who use their knives daily are the W.R. Case & Sons "Case/Ruple Axe Handle" folder designed by Bill Ruple, the Halfbreed Blades CQC-025 Karambit, Bear Ops "Double Clutch IV" auto and Kansept "Link" frame-lock folder.

Three more "Blue-Collar Blades" include the CobraTec "Surgeon" neck knife, A.G. Russell Knives "Power Ball 4" folder, and Fox Cutlery "Anzu" Verso Lock folding knife.

“Duo Desk Knife” (dual knives with neodymium magnets), the Condor Tool & Knife “Narrowsaur” Scandinavian-ground fixed blade, and Bradford USA’s “Gatsby Steak Knife.”

« Some nice, new factory knives include the QSP Knife "Turtle Punk" named for the black-and-white-patterned G-10 handle, the Reate Knives "GTR" flipper folder, Smoky Mountain Knife Works "Rough Ryder Reserve Hawkeye" with hawk-bill blade and the SOG Tech Bowie.

Rounding out the Blue-Collar Blades are a Benchmade "99 Necron" Balisong, Spartan Blades "Clandestina" designed by Bill Harsey Jr. and a Cold Steel "AD-10 Ti Limited Edition" drop-point folder.

FRAME-LOCK FOLDERS

Modern frame-lock folders entering the fray, from top to bottom, are the Kershaw "Helitack," CRKT "Padawan," Bastinelli "BBR2," and Hinderer Knives "Halftrack."

CRESCENT CUTTERS—MODERN KARAMBITS

Modern Karambit models come in such packages as the Boker Plus "HEL Karambit" (shown in black and gray versions), the RMJ Tactical "Korbin," Halfbreed Blades "CQC-02 Close Quarters Combat" and CobraTec "OD Green Double Action."

TRUSTWORTHY EDCS

Built for everyday carry are the Hogue Knives "Mysto," Kershaw "Bel Air," Bear Ops "Rancor IX," Maserin "Power," A.G. Russell Knives "Power Ball 4," and Fox Cutlery "ATCF Original Gangster."

Filling a niche for EDC folders are the Cold Steel "Caledonian," Coast Cutlery "Founder's Series Origin," and Queen Cutlery "SlipJoint Pocketknife."

Rounding out a plethora of factory everyday carry folders are the Alliance Designs “EZE 2.0,” Blackbird Products “Dominator,” and Reate Knives “PL-XT.”

POPULAR PUUKKO KNIVES

Four stellar puukkos are, from left to right, the Reiff Knives "F4 Scandi Bushcraft," Marttiini "Arctic Bush Knife," Bear Forest Knives "Simple 3," and Morakniv "Classic No. 1/0.

KNIFEMAKERS INDEX

DOTS GEAR
Locked in. Game on.
No matter what you need,
DOTS GEAR keeps ready for anything.
MAGNACUT
Diafire
Saffire
TAC
www.dots-us.com | sales@dots-us.com

Reate
KNIVES
Terminator-T600
Blade length: 3.8"
Open Length: 9"
Handle: Titanium-bead blasted
Weight:11oz
Blade: Magnacut/Frosted satin
Clip: Zirconium-green
Pivot Collar: Zirconium-green
VK-TRON
Blade length: 3.3"
Opening Method: Flipper
Open Length: 7.8"
Handle: Titanium-bead blasted with pattern
Weight:4.4oz
Blade: M390/Darkwashed
Clip: Crystalized Titanium-gray
Pivot Collar: Crystalized Titanium-gray
VK-ANUB
Blade length: 3.15"
Opening Method: Front Flipper
Open Length: 7.48"
Handle:Titanium-Bead blast
Weight:3.35oz
Blade: Elmax/Hand rubbed
Clip:Titanium-satin
reateknives
sales@reateknives.com
www.reateknives.com

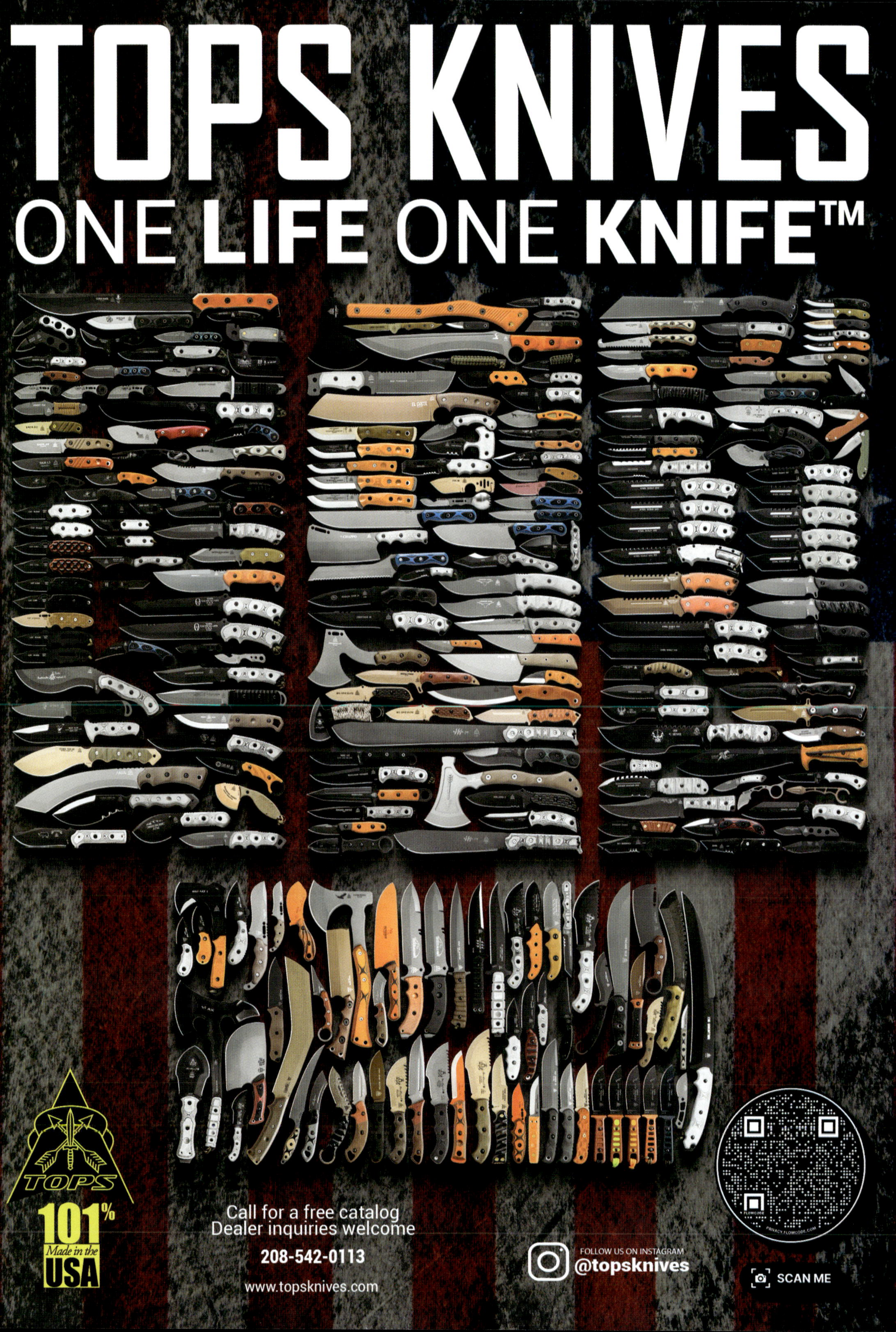

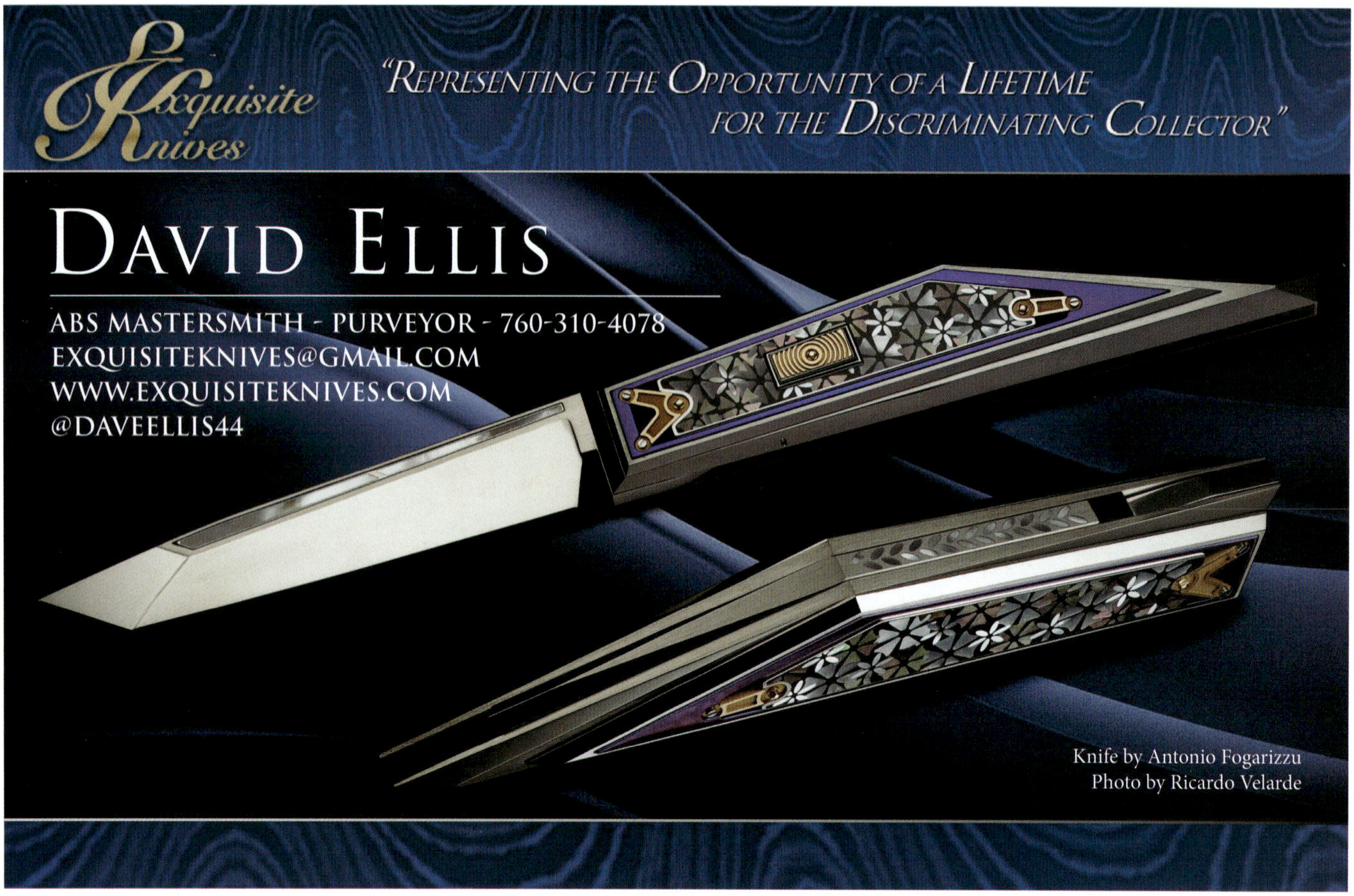
Exquisite Knives
"Representing the Opportunity of a Lifetime for the Discriminating Collector"
DAVID ELLIS
ABS MASTERSMITH - PURVEYOR - 760-310-4078
EXQUISITEKNIVES@GMAIL.COM
WWW.EXQUISITEKNIVES.COM
@DAVEELLIS44
Knife by Antonio Fogarizzu
Photo by Ricardo Velarde

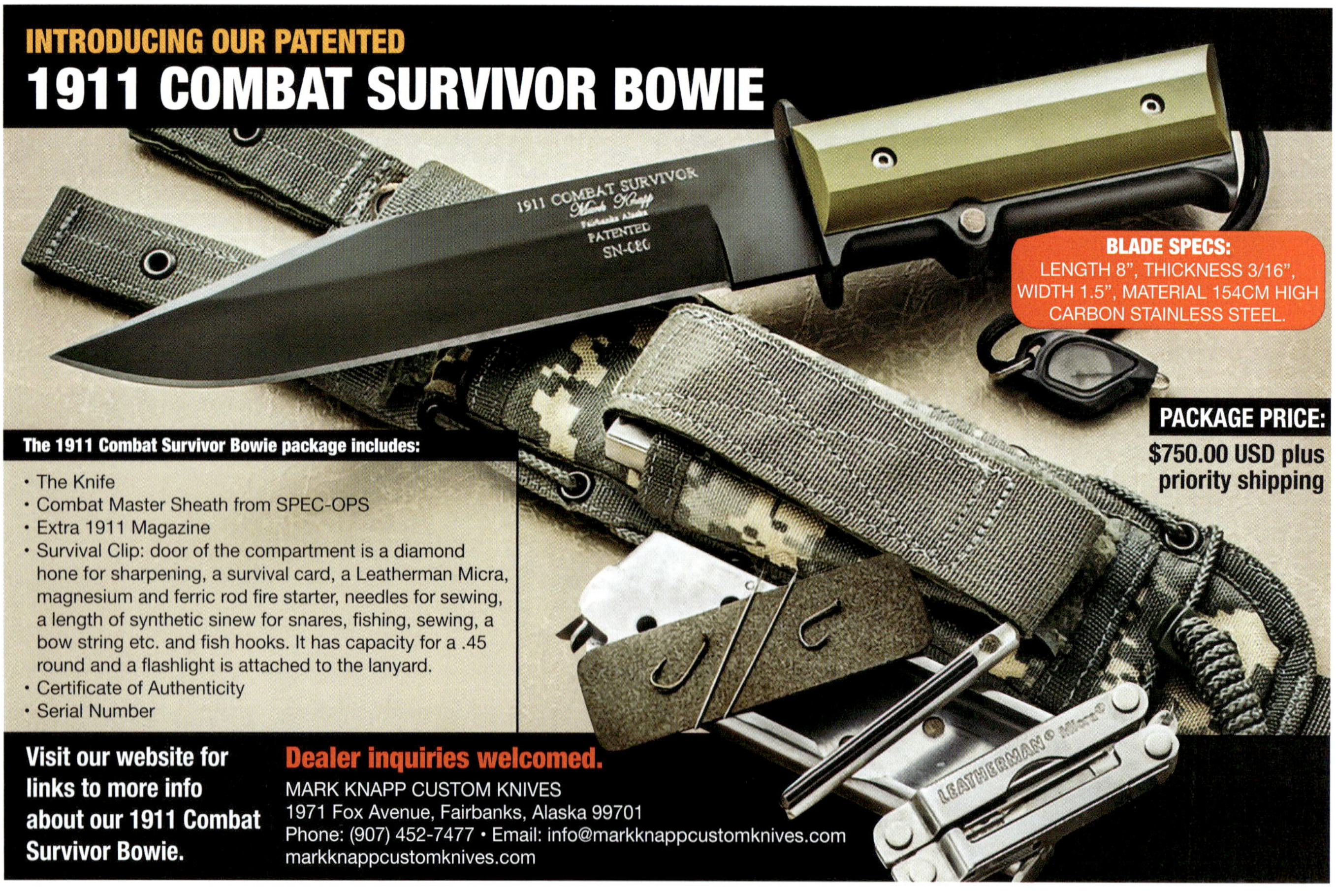
INTRODUCING OUR PATENTED
1911 COMBAT SURVIVOR BOWIE
1911 COMBAT SURVIVOR
Fairbanks Alaska
PATENTED
SN-080
BLADE SPECS:
LENGTH 8", THICKNESS 3/16", WIDTH 1.5", MATERIAL 154CM HIGH CARBON STAINLESS STEEL.
PACKAGE PRICE:
$750.00 USD plus priority shipping
The 1911 Combat Survivor Bowie package includes:
• The Knife
• Combat Master Sheath from SPEC-OPS
• Extra 1911 Magazine
• Survival Clip: door of the compartment is a diamond hone for sharpening, a survival card, a Leatherman Micra, magnesium and ferric rod fire starter, needles for sewing, a length of synthetic sinew for snares, fishing, sewing, a bow string etc. and fish hooks. It has capacity for a .45 round and a flashlight is attached to the lanyard.
• Certificate of Authenticity
• Serial Number
Visit our website for links to more info about our 1911 Combat Survivor Bowie.
Dealer inquiries welcomed.
MARK KNAPP CUSTOM KNIVES
1971 Fox Avenue, Fairbanks, Alaska 99701
Phone: (907) 452-7477 • Email: info@markknappcustomknives.com
markknappcustomknives.com
LEATHERMAN Micra

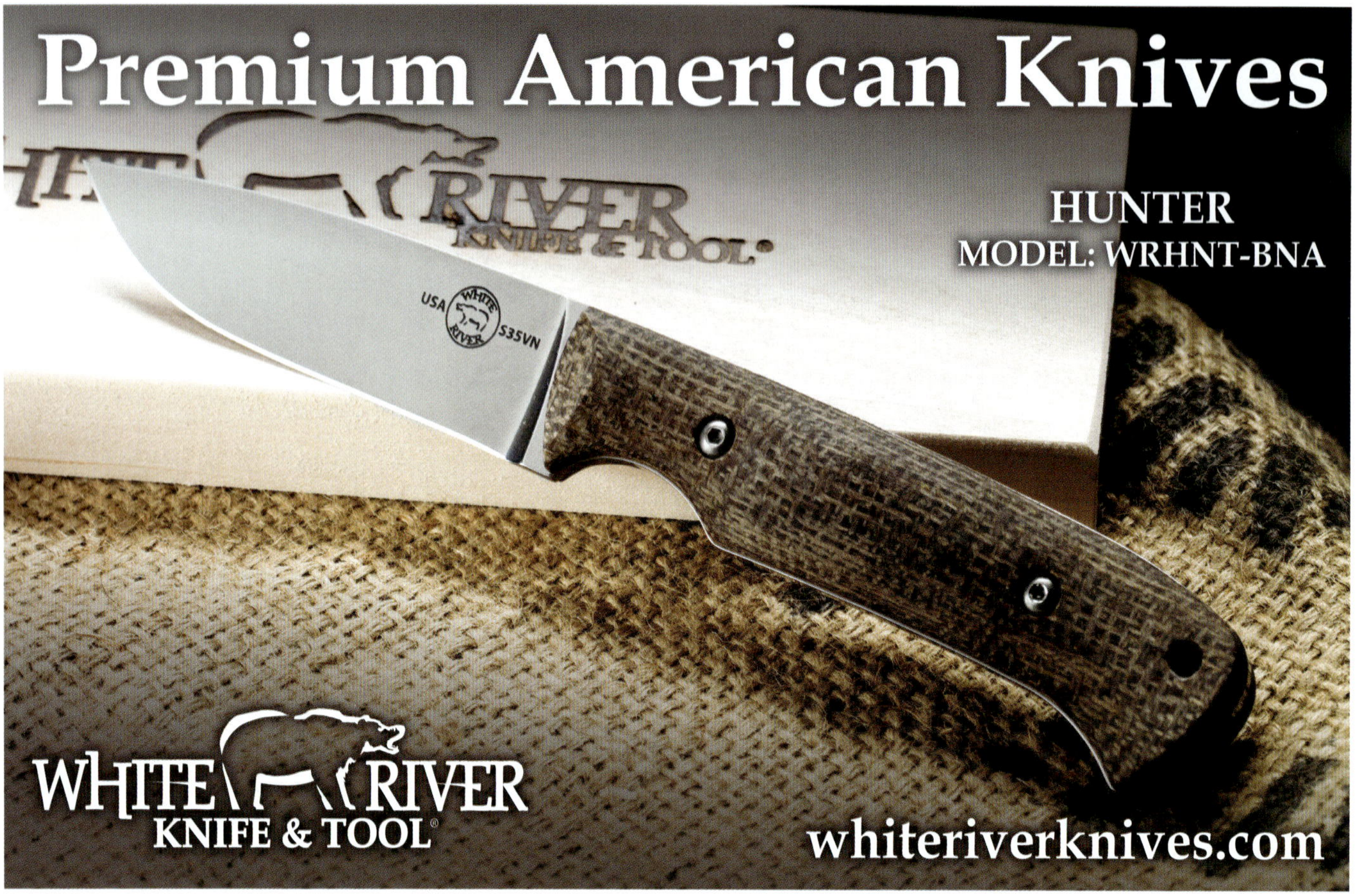
Premium American Knives
HUNTER
MODEL: WRHNT-BNA
USA WHITE RIVER S35VN
WHITE RIVER
KNIFE & TOOL®
whiteriverknives.com

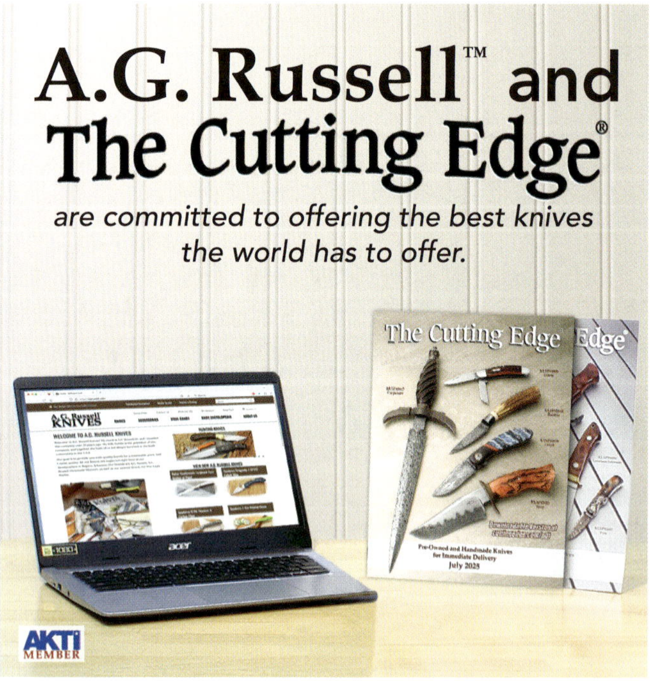
A.G. Russell™ and
The Cutting Edge®
are committed to offering the best knives the world has to offer.
The Cutting Edge
Pre-Owned and Handmade Knives for Immediate Delivery
July 2025
acer
AKTI MEMBER

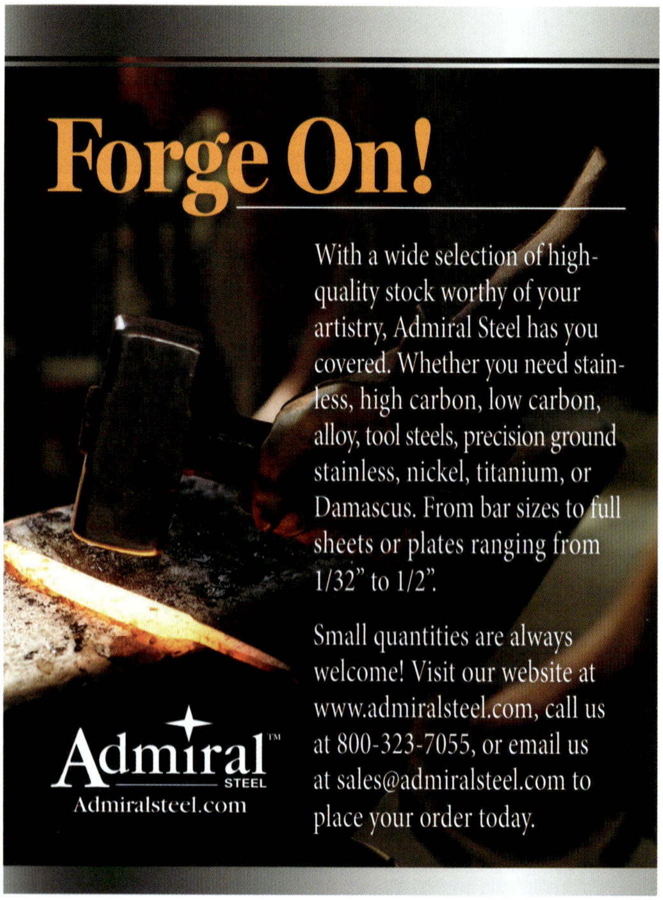
Forge On!
With a wide selection of high-quality stock worthy of your artistry, Admiral Steel has you covered. Whether you need stainless, high carbon, low carbon, alloy, tool steels, precision ground stainless, nickel, titanium, or Damascus. From bar sizes to full sheets or plates ranging from 1/32" to 1/2".
Small quantities are always welcome! Visit our website at www.admiralsteel.com, call us at 800-323-7055, or email us at sales@admiralsteel.com to place your order today.
Admiral™ STEEL
Admiralsteel.com

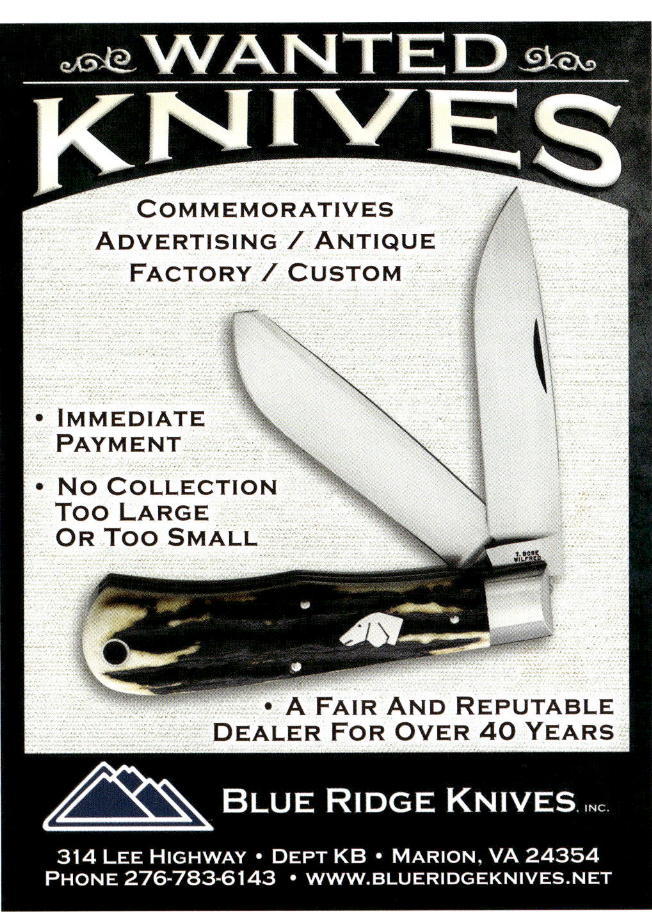
WANTED
KNIVES
Commemoratives
Advertising / Antique
Factory / Custom
• Immediate Payment
• No Collection Too Large Or Too Small
• A Fair And Reputable Dealer For Over 40 Years
Blue Ridge Knives, inc.
314 Lee Highway • Dept KB • Marion, VA 24354
Phone 276-783-6143 • www.blueridgeknives.net

Chris Reeve Knives
CHRISREEVE.COM
CPM® MAGNACUT
PACIFIC
CPM® MAGNACUT
GREEN BERET

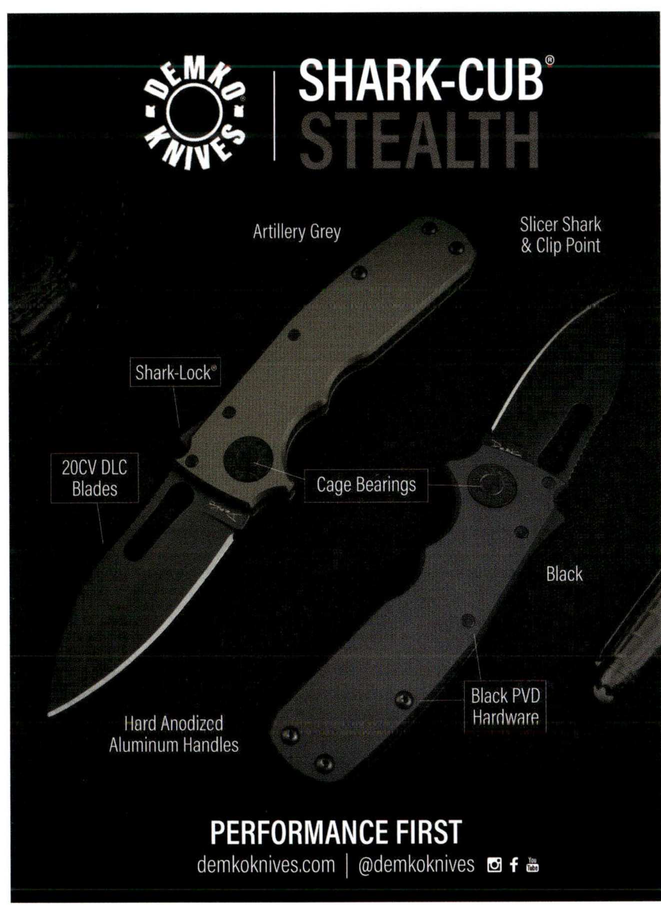
DEMKO KNIVES
SHARK-CUB®
STEALTH
Artillery Grey
Slicer Shark & Clip Point
Shark-Lock®
20CV DLC Blades
Cage Bearings
Black
Black PVD Hardware
Hard Anodized Aluminum Handles
PERFORMANCE FIRST
demkoknives.com | @demkoknives

evenheat

SUBSCRIBE TODAY!

NEW SUBSCRIBERS:
BladeMag.com/subscribe

TO RENEW:
BladeMag.com/renew